一位美轮美奂的
小诗人之歌

Songs of a Resplendent Minor Poet

by Lu Jian

陆健 著

Tr. by Denis Mair

梅丹理 译

易文出版社 · 纽约

I Wing Press, New York

Songs of a Resplendent Minor Poet
by Lu Jian
Tr. by Denis Mair
一位美轮美奂的小诗人之歌
陆健 著
梅丹理 译
ISBN：978-1-961768-24-6

Table of Contents

目　录

POETRY

1. I said to myself, Guillaume, it's time you came
   --- *(Guillaume Apollinaire)* 2

2. I am nobody, who are you?
   --- *(Emily Dickinson)* 4

3. After wearing out ten thousand books, my brush is moved
   as if by spirits   --- *(Du Fu, Tang era)* 6

4. She was like an angel from Heaven, descending to show us
   miracles   --- *(Dante)* 8

5. They sewed fig leaves together and made coverings
   for themselves   --- *(Holy Bible, Old Testament)* 10

6. Essays should be dedicated to an era; poems should be created
   for an occasion   --- *(Bai Juyin, Tang)* 12

7. With the aid of Athena, Achilles drove his spear through
   Hector's neck   --- *(Illiad, Book 22)* 14

8. With sadness I survey our present generation
   --- *(Lermontov)* 16

9. If only my heart is upright, even remoteness is of no concern.
   --- *(Qu Yuan, "Crossing the River")* 18

10. Live where you live
    --- *(Hjalmar Guldberg, Sweden)* 20

11. We are all responsible to all for all
    --- *(Dostoevsky)* 22

12. The reason I have great affliction is that I have a body
     --- *(Lao Tzu)*   24

13. You who write, choose a subject suitable to your abilities
     --- *(Horace, "Ars Poetica")*   26

14. The spellbound heart has made and remade the necklace
     of songs   ---*(Tagore, "Unending Love")*   28

15. The Chinese Nation Is at Its Time of Greatest Danger
     --- *(Tian Han, "March of Volunteer Warriors"--China's national anthem)* 30

16. In This Era, What Is a Poet For
     ---*(Heidegger)*   32

17. We choose what we will make ourselves to be
     ---*(Sartre, "Existentialism Is a Humanism")*   34

18. Cut bamboo, assemble bamboo, make clay pellets,
     chase living flesh
     --- *("Crossbow Song"---an ancient song of the Spring Autumn Period)* 36

19. The world is a stage, but the play is badly cast
     --- *(Oscar Wilde, "Lord Savile's Crime")*   38

20. We only enjoy the happiness we are able to understand
     --- *(Maeterlinck, "The Blue Bird")*   40

21. Each day I reflect three times on my conduct
     ---*(Zengzi, Analects)*   42

22. Be less curious about people and more curious about ideas
     --- *(Madame Curie)*   44

23. My aspiration was to become a minor poet, and I've succeeded.
     --- *(Borges)*   46

24. Plucking mums beneath the eastern hedge, I serenely
     gaze at mountains to the south   --- *(Tao Yuanming)*   48

25. You will not stumble if you choose the path
     --- *(Egypt, The Book of Going forth by Day)*   50

26. ...and miles to go before I sleep and miles to go before I sleep
     ---*(Robert Frost)*   52

ESSAYS

Lu Jian's Inner Journey in Poetry   *By Shan Zhansheng*   55

A Long Masterwork of Contemporary Chinese Poetry
     —*A Brief Discussion on "Songs of a Resplendent
     Minor Poet"*   *by Xiong Guohua*   74

A Dantesque Questioning and Redemption in the Wasteland
     of the Soul—*A Draft Essay on Lu Jian's Long Poem
     "Songs of a Resplendent Minor Poet"*   *by Zi Wu*   85

Works That Can Destroy Their Authors
     —*Afterword to the Poetry Collection
     "Songs of a Resplendent Minor Poet"*   *Lu Jian*   113

诗 歌 篇

1. 我对自己说吉约姆是你来的时候了
    ——（法）吉约姆·阿波利奈   128

2. 我是无名之辈，你是谁？
    ——（美）狄金森   130

3. 读书破万卷，下笔如有神
    ——（中）杜甫   132

4. 她恍若上界的一位天使，降临人间把奇迹向我们显示
    ——（意）但丁   134

5. 他们急忙摘下一些无花果叶盖住身体
    ——（古希伯来《旧约全书》）   136

6. 文章合为时而著，歌诗合为事而作
    ——（中）白居易   138

7. 在雅典娜的帮助下，阿喀琉斯一挥长矛正中赫克托尔的颈项
　　——（古希腊）荷马　140

8. 我悲哀地看着我们这一代人
　　——（俄）莱蒙托夫　142

9. 苟余心之端直兮，虽僻远其何伤？
　　——（中）屈原　144

10. 生存在你所生存的地方
　　——（瑞典）古尔贝里　146

11. 每个人都应该对世上一切人和一切事物负责
　　——（俄）陀思妥耶夫斯基　148

12. 吾所以有大患者，为吾有身
　　——（中）老子　150

13. 写作要选取适合自己的题材
　　——（古罗马）贺拉斯　152

14. 爱的欢乐只能用艺术的形式来表达
　　——（印）泰戈尔　154

15. 中华民族到了最危险的时候
　　——（中）田汉　156

16. 在今天的时代，诗人何为？
　　——（德）海德格尔　158

17. 你选择什么样的存在，完全取决于自己
　　——（法）萨特　160

18. 断竹，续竹，飞土，逐肉
　　——（中）《上古歌谣·弹歌》　162

19. 这世界就是舞台，可角色分配得不像样子
　　——（英）王尔德　164

20. 我们只能享有我们所能理解的幸福
　　——（比）梅特林克　　　　　　　　　166

21. 吾日三省吾身
　　——（中）曾子　　　　　　　　　　　168

22. 荣誉就像玩具，只能玩玩而已
　　——（波）居里夫人　　　　　　　　　170

23. 我的志愿就是作一个小诗人，而我早已到达
　　——（阿根廷）博尔赫斯　　　　　　　172

24. 采菊东篱下，悠然见南山
　　——（中）陶渊明　　　　　　　　　　174

25. 你再没有可能被绊倒，在你自行选择的小径上
　　——（古埃及）《亡灵书》　　　　　　176

26. 天黑前路途遥遥，天黑前路途遥遥
　　——（美）弗罗斯特　　　　　　　　　178

评　论　篇

陆健诗歌的心路历程　　　单占生　　　　　　181

中国当代诗坛的长篇杰作
　　——简论《一位美轮美奂的小诗人之歌》　熊国华　197

心灵荒原的"但丁式"拷问与救赎
　　——陆健长诗《一位美轮美奂的小诗人之歌》论稿　子　午　206

那些能够杀伤作者的作品
　　——诗集《一位美轮美奂的小诗人之歌》代后记　陆　健　230

POETRY

1.   I said to myself, Guillaume, it's time you came

--- *(Guillaume Apollinaire)*

A. If Apollinaire could come, of course I can come

It is my vocation to create an image of a contemporary poet
Hundreds of times I must break it apart and shape myself
Countless were those who came down through the ages

of whom many comers would never disappear again
There was a time they wept, laughed, rejoiced, despaired
they came to worry for us or ridicule us. They are our relations

yet have nothing to do with us. They loom over us, stern and aloof
sometimes even leaking away between our fingers
The language they used fills our mouths

a. The Implications of "I"

I am just myself, not the I of yesterday
not the future I, not an idea of self
not a definition, but a fleshly body

You may say my skull is made of iron
my torso and hands are wood, my legs

shaped from terra cotta, in surprise I beg to differ

My physique is normal for an Asian man
except for being soft-hearted, every inch
is taut and firm; my fertility is undiminished

My staple foods are flour, rice and corn
along with Confucian and Taoist writings
In translation I savor bread and Western culture

I am a product of agrarian ways, swept up
by machines and pushed headlong towards computers
taking care to protect my delicate lower ribs

In front of others I magnify my strengths
I am an enemy of tyranny, and at the same time
a kindhearted adherent of Tolstoy's thought

2. I am nobody, who are you?

--- (Emily Dickinson)

B. Laurels

Among Tang poets there was a Li Bai ("Li the White")
who could just as well have been Li the Black, and in our time
Gao Xingjian [1] could have been French, and what would it matter?

Back in the time when Nobel first offered his prize
he did it because none of that matters. For thousands of years
the writings people left to us were one great work

The laurel that crowned Homer was handed down in relay
to crown another Homer. He himself would never see
that laurel crown, what he saw was his own inner darkness

[1] Gao Xingjian 高行健 was the first Chinese writer to win the Nobel Prize, in 2000. An excellent French translation of his novel *Soul Mountain*, done by Liliane and Noël Dutrait, helped to win the attention of the judging committee.

b. Who Would It Be Better to Be?

My upper lip quivers, says, nothing to do with me
my lower lip is quick to negate... Who should I be?
I want to see recompense in this lifetime

If I would be like Dickinson, might as well not write
I can become a four star chef, learn to roast duck
make it crisp and tender to sell at a good price

People lead busy lives. A national chairman keeps busy
just as cobbler keeps busy. You might as well make it count
That is the philosophy I've subscribed to since childhood

Jesus upholds tolerance, but it is not clear to me
if I have a place under his eaves of tolerance or not
Does His benevolence illuminate the ancient Orient?

I know what I am doing, or maybe I don't know
CHANGES OF ZHOU... day one in a cycle,
an encompassing compass, recurrent round of rebirth [1]

Now I'm huge and now tiny; in youth not seeing much
at forty still bewildered; at fifty not knowing heaven's command [2]
living on and on until I've lived myself...into the shape I'm in

---

[1] The earliest known title of the classical text *BOOK OF CHANGES* was "Changes of Zhou" (周易 *Zhōuyì*), so-named because it was compiled in the Zhou era. The title *Zhōuyì* sounds like the words *zhōu-yī* 周一 ("embracing and unified" or "Day One of a weekly cycle"). The compound word *yuán-zhōu* 圓周 literally means "round and encompassing." The phrase *zhōu-ér-fù-shǐ* 周而复始 means "recurring" or literally "circling back to its beginnings"). All of these expressions include the word zhou 周, which was the name of the dynasty in which the schools of classical Chinese philosophy emerged.

[2] Here Lu Jian plays upon a famous quotation from Confucius summarized his personal development in these words: "...at forty I was not bewildered, and at fifty I knew Heaven's command..."

3. After wearing out ten thousand books,
    my brush is moved as if by spirits
    --- *(Du Fu, Tang era)*

C. Neither a Brush Nor a Quill

My left hand grasps poetry, my right hand takes hold of reality
I write poems by transposing music and generating images
at times like taking dictation, now and then by flash of inspiration

Where the past masters left off, there my writing commences
Since the time of Baudelaire we've done things this way
Even though I know I am still a minor figure

I got the food and clothes a child needs to grow, and my lower body
swelled along with my intellect, whereupon I devoured masses of books
until fingers dancing on keys took the place of writing by hand

c. We Poets of This Era

Old Du had his own path; Gu Cheng had his consummate moves
like in volleyball, the ball is fed to the one who sets pen to paper
so Du Fu's striking spot was always within bounds of classicism

Looking at you there's a distance, looking up at clouds I feel nearness

which hints at a choice of subjects, from far outside to near and inside
then set up your position so you can slip in for stunning effect**

Among poets of our era, those with long necks were called
Young A, Young B, Young C, Young D; those with shorter necks
were called Cat, Dog, Little Fish or Little Shrimp. At first

we went naked, making a ruckus all day long, then later
when our voices changed, we abruptly ran off in all directions
No one was able to call anyone else by name. From then on

strange events happened frequently...at the most agonizing
or most joyful moments, we'd let out a yell, only to hear
someone's voice responding. Some say that a robust Yu Jian

lurks in the mind of Xi Chuan. How could that be? And some say
an upended Xi Chuan hangs in Yu Jian's heart, which seems an affront
but to mention a touch of jealousy would not be going too far

4. She was like an angel from Heaven,

descending to show us miracles

--- (Dante)

D. Dante and Poker

Dante stands at the apex of an "A", gazing down on humans
on their paths of living and dying; I stand in the trough of a "V"
sunk in an abyss, calling out right and left for rescue

Our self redemption is like a poker game lit by hearth-light
played by knights in a gothic castle along the Rhine
You call for Rilke, he throws down the Derrida card

Wittgenstein gains the upper hand, being held by Young "B"
China's sun was blocked by a demon screen…we were careless
and became fond of pre-paid cards from Carrefour and KFC [1]

[1] During the 2000s and the -10s, the Chinese government encouraged large
foreign franchise networks to set up joint ventures, including the French Carrefour
chain, which operated shopping emporiums similar to America's Costco. In the late
-10s, China suddenly withdrew licenses from the Carrefour stores. People who had
bought pre-paid purchase cards were left in the lurch.

d. Banana Co-Living Flats and a Master's Knit Brow

Some say I'm too serious, putting on airs of a foreign literary figure
I paste quotes from Western thinkers on the walls of my flat
and peer at the world from behind the shoulders of a master

Some meet with well-known figures in the pages of my works
and think they must doff their caps each time. Some say my face
is a painting without expression; I parade it about using my neck

to hold it up. My Sinitic language is mixed with phonetic spellings
due to an innate sense of lack, I cannot help being like this
Excuse me, Mr. James will honor my humble room with a visit soon

Some say not only poets are like this; fiction writers are moreso
The length of their works is custom tailored to certain occasions
For instance, the punctuation of *Old Man and the Sea* in English

is copied out first, only then are the blanks filled in with Chinese
so someday Goeran Malmqvist will pound the table in approval
at such profundity, and while judging give it a crucial vote

Someone once said that poetry is what is lost in translation, but perhaps
the biggest knack lies in luring translators to flaunt their embroidery
"Excuse me, Mr. James is already knocking at my door"

5.   They sewed fig leaves together
and made coverings for themselves

--- (Holy Bible, Old Testament)

E. Leaves and Fruits

The first right given to humankind in the Garden of Eden
was the right to privacy. Adam and Eve used fig leaves to cover
their nakedness. The counter-culture is first to oppose fig leaves

People who study culture often indulge in sexual fantasies
In rural towns there's a buzz over sex toys; some websites
host naked chatrooms; summer fashions reveal midribs and buttocks

Women's skirts get shorter and shorter…redefining beauty
Scientific intellect invents refrigeration techniques
to preserve the freshness' of stale old stories

e. How Far Can a Poem Take Us?

How far can a poem take us? Or should I say
what is our distance from a poem? Wait a minute
I forgot to return a beautiful woman's phone call

Incoming: 3.1415926, an eight digit number, clearly someone

calling from a major city. The voice message is brief
not putting pressure on me, a sign of good upbringing

With poetry in the lead we can head off anywhere
but for her rations she'll consume our life force
Due to rejection of that reality I had to suppress her

I set forth from a village, without really knowing
what I was after. One way or another I would need to eat
so good food would be best; I would need to wear clothes

so name brands would be best; I'd need to go after a woman
so a pretty one would be best, or I'd need to have a pretty one
come after me. So I thought I'd try going after poetry first

In the face of utter materialism, it is the human spirit's lot in life
to be raped. Our fates ordain that some people will applaud this
but laughter over such things is what I relish like dessert

6.   Essays should be dedicated to an era;
poems should be created for an occasion

--- (Bai Juyin, Tang)

F. Who Has Died for Me? For Whom Will I Die?

Lu Ban the legendary craftsman died for Bill Gates; Su Dongpo died
to make way for poets like Huang Tingjian; and Jorge Luis Borges—
for the sake of light—had to lose his penetrating eyesight

Soldiers died for generals, the living died so coffins would be made
Who cares if handiworks will rust? Anyway history needs to be judged,
words need to be polished. Living to write is at least as hard

as making love, and the effort has to be an all-out endeavor
Even if the world has been patched together into a flat face
it is a poet's fate to be the nose that stands out

f. Writing in the Age of We-Chat

Strange to say, my computer finds it hard to input the words
"WeChat"--preferring to leave all the ceaseless messaging
to owners of other terminals, along busy avenues

and to teen-aged girls with heads lowered on public buses

Yesterday a friend said to me, "I want to flag you"［夹你 *jiá nǐ*］
I shot back: "You want to 'friend me,'［加我 *jiā wǒ*］, not 'flag me'"

"Beginning tomorrow, I will be a poet too," I said
"I have no doubt you will." In fact, I was preoccupied
And remembered something that happened over a late lunch—

A friend made an introduction: "This is a poet." The top official
twitched his brows, one thick and one thin, and the boss
turned up the corners of his mouth, one lower one higher

In my torso I felt the a grand afflatus churning
it almost vented, but I nodded with a discrete air
more of a gentleman than usual. Ah Poetry

once the God of morality set His sights on her
now yielding sovereignty to the God of commerce
she suffers the torment of a thousand cuts for us

7.   With the aid of Athena,
Achilles drove his spear through Hector's neck
--- (Illiad, Book 22)

G. Achilles' Spear Struck with the Strength of Homer's Arm

Written words, like human beings, can be cured by bloodletting
Poetry's axe chops down, words bleed at that moment
they bleed as I fall over, which is made known by swirling dust

With a thrust of his spear, Achilles ended Hector's life
WWII's sweeping broom heightened mankind's sense of peril
Einstein made the rationale of space conform to a curve

Ideology ascends in a spiral... nationalities, states, isms
schools and techniques of poetry vs. its essence and principles
whorls that took shape on my palmprint, in the name of freedom

g. How Big a Problem Can a Generation Solve?

I've eaten a thousand bowls of rice, and fitted a frame of aluminum
to a Rembrandt painting; I have taken one hundred showers
and dipped the wolf hair brush of Huang Binhong in ink

He knew how to let in a streak of light into a landscape
Just when Bada Shanren's birdsong was being heard
twilight was causing T.S. Eliot to fain away

Usain Bolt cut 0.16 seconds from Asafa Powell's record
but philosophers turn back to study Lao Tzu's sublimity
Across my desk are spread 17 editions of *Tao-teh Ching*

The crane arm of time swings, perhaps history precedes
and the future is behind, or perhaps the other way around
perhaps I've spent a lifetime making one mistake

My light source is a 60 watt bulb and my eyesight is suited
to 30 watts. Nausea is a phone call from someone
It's late at night and the number is not in my "Contacts"

As usual my girlfriend stretches her neck while taking a pill
she makes a loud, ruffling sound while changing bedsheets
and the look she gives me is fraught with ambiguity

8. With sadness I survey our present generation
--- (Lermontov)

H. With Sadness Our Generation Surveys Lermontov

Academic shows, reality shows, showmanship, parody shows
shows of eloquence and tongue-tied shows
Put on a ruminative look, a look of absurd imagining

Act like the left and right body halves are unmatched, or act
like a greenhorn, like you're cool or stylish, act like a dead dog
give it a poke and it will slink away over a wall

I took birth from my swaddling clothes, not from mother's body
my intellect comes from truth and not from life
with sadness our present generation surveys Lermontov

h. The Sunflower Manual for Winning Instant Fame

Step 1: Give myself a distinctive pen name
A poet in Shanghai thought of naming himself "Waibai" [1]
and his poet-girlfriend named herself "Duqiao" [2]

Step 2: Starting at a top school, treat poetry as a movement
then stir up a big splash to make my name a hot commodity

which will appear in big journals, weeklies and anthologies

Step 3: Don't offend leaders or plain folk. As the scene unravels
rummage through trash and weeds; then when I become famous
wield a scalpel-like pen, noting all the details to expose gross faults

Step 4: Study a foreign language. Even if I murder the pronunciation
my poems will conform to European syntax, for ease of translation
Best of all, have Mr. Li Li hand deliver them to contacts in Stockholm [3]

Step 5: Stand beside people who have hulking, strapping physiques
When people see them, they will notice me there
They'll see embroidery; at the same time they'll see plain stitches

Step 6: Set myself in opposition to a certain now-deceased figure
Of course I'll appear as one whose intentions are wholly innocent
The heart bent on grand success has the focus of a fine needle

[1] [2] In Shanghai the first bridge to span the Soochow River was the Wills
Bridge (Garden Bridge) built in 1873, rebuilt in 1906, and rebuilt again in 1946. Its
Chinese name is *Waibai-duqiao* 外白渡橋 (literally "White-Beyond Crossing Bridge").
The two pen names Waibai and Duqiao are coined by splitting the bridge's name in
half.

[3] The Chinese poet Li Li 李笠 studied Swedish in college and worked on the
Swedish language edition of *Beijing Review*. He married a woman who holds a position
in the Swedish Foreign Service, and Li Li sometimes accompanies her to foreign
postings as a diplomat's spouse.

9.　If only my heart is upright,

even remoteness is of no concern.

--- (Qu Yuan, "Crossing the River")

I. Contemporary Beauty Is Fast-Paced

In Qu Yuan's songs, beauty is tied to an ill-fated kingdom and its king
Death becomes beauty; things that reach extremes have beauty hiding
in them, the edge of a sword's blade, the foot of Cinderella

the round edge of Venus' severed arm, a lovely face that waited
to outgrow freckles; a lame horse that was cured became
a fine steed, an end to affliction by cold sores and stuttering

Yet flowers cannot protect their scent, the beauty of poppies
decrees they must grow somewhere secluded; the trailing curls
of a long-bearded violinist will someday snap his neck

i. Language in Costume

I often think the authors of　*Book of Songs* and "Ode to an Orange"[1]
were making fun of current writers; in fact when writing those odes,
they had no time to find fault; they were simply fond of nouns

As for Tang poets— their talent lay in aestheticism, like a bevy of maids

busily attending to their mistress' toilette, applying foundation and rouge
using adjectives as ornament to heighten the elegance of words

to such a painstaking degree they nearly got on their mistress' nerves.
Later literati took the lessons to heart, and learned them with a vengeance
They fed language so much candy its nouns suffered tooth decay

even giving their subjects breast enlargements and tissue grafts
or reconstructive surgery, slicing and dicing concepts, like food courts
that serve "fried ice cream." For instance ideas of "nation" and "state"

once two distinct terms, are mingling currents like Jing and Wei rivers
Now even words like "way" and "principle" have a homoerotic fling [2]
from "the knight on yonder bank" to a "murky mingling of waters"

I hear my landlord secretly stifling a laugh, and I imagine the sight
Of Jia Sidao [3], who once showed up at *levée* in a courtier's robe,
under which he wore one shoe of his own, one of his gay lover.

[1] The *Book of Odes* was authored by anonymous singers of the Zhou Dynasty. The "Ode to Oranges" was in the collection *Songs of the South*, by Qu Yuan of the Chu Kingdom (also in the Zhou era). In both books the language was relatively unadorned and straightforward compared to the Tang era.

[2] The word "Way" (*dao* 道) is a key concept in Taoism, and the word "principle" (*li* 理) was a key term in Confucianism from the Song era on.

[3] Jia Sidao (1213-1275) was an influential court minister of the Song era. The anecdote about him appearing at court in mismatched shoes reveals his homosexual tendencies.

10. Live where you live

--- *(Hjalmar Guldberg, Sweden)*

J. Not in Changping, Not in Xining

Not just Chang Yao,[1] not just Haizi,[2] not in a flat in Changping [3]
not beside Qinghai Lake [4] where dogbane grows, Beijing also needs
someone to keep a vigil, to penetrate the world's vitals with his gaze

Beneath the arches of my feet, the subducted stratum needs to hold firm
As I reach out, is it to take something for myself,
or is it to hand over what is needed by another person?

In a flash of thought, in calendar pages eaten by silverfish larvae
in ledgers, in manuals, while making my way through a crowd
holding chalk in curled fingers, I come to Dingfu-zhuang E. Road [5]

Notes:

[1][2][3][4] The common feature of these poets and places is their distance from
Beijing. Xining is the capital of Qinghai Province. Chang Yao (1936-2000) was a poet
from Hunan who was exiled to Qinghai Province during the Anti-Rightist Campaign
of the Fifties. He married a Tibetan woman and spent almost twenty years in a
remote setting. In the 1980s he was vindicated and inducted into the Writers
Association. Many consider him to be the most   famous poet of Qinghai.// Haizi
(1964-1989) was an active poet at Beijing University in the Eighties. In the last years
of his life he travelled restlessly. He is remembered as a tragic figure due to his suicide
in 1989. Haizi's connection to Qinghai Province is tenuous, but in 1988 he traveled
to Delingha in north-central Qinghai. Changping is in the distant northwest suburbs
outside of Beijing. It has now been incorporated into the city.

[5] This is the address of China Communications University, the largest media
studies institution in China, where the poet taught for many years.

j. My Insistent Love and My Life's Concreteness

My insistent love and life's concreteness
demand that I won't pickle my loneliness in drink
and then spout massive rants of dream babble

My eyes are on my payslip: one is one, two is two
My vicinity lacks contact with expansive, rugged nature
Haizi's territory and commitment show me no favor

My principle: do not take phone calls from others
In case I do, if direct refusal is not fitting
gaze out the window or at my lowered eyelids

Do not step up to help my boss earn money, even if he's a boss
who is merely "purveying desolation"[1], because in my eyes
"desolation" is a just a warrior who has yet to make his debut

How I wish for vaulting skies and hazy wild views, for a carefree life
open to the light, but my son is growing and spring is losing weight
I can only tug at her bedraggled sleeve, using my hands

that grip handlebars tightly on my way to work, my hands
that caressed a young woman into a matron showing her age
But how could I ever make this an excuse for compromise?

[1] The idea of "purveying desolation" has been used in magazines to describe
the investment activities of the writer Zhang Xianliang, who in 1993 began
converting the ruins of an old fort town in Ningxia to a film lot and later into
"Zhenbeibao," a tourist destination for movie lovers.

11. We are all responsible to all for all

--- *(Dostoevsky)* [1]

K. Free or Not Free of Responsibility

Some people are responsible to all for all, but not responsible
to themselves; some take no responsibility to anyone but themselves
This morning at a hospital drop-in, the doctor said I was responsible

for the cryptic cystitis in my belly, but he would only be responsible
for receipt of payments. At dusk in the park my "her" stifled sobs
because love can no longer be responsible for virginity

Poets are responsible for the psoriasis of words and phrases
for when the spleen and gall of language are unwell, and when
its diet is unvaried, leading to osteoporosis and chronic debility

[1]This quote was spoken by the character Father Zossima in "Chapter 40" of
Dostoevsky's novel *The Brothers Karamazov.*

k. Poetry and the "Usefulness of Expediency"

Names of persons, varieties of flowers, "Yellow Crane" rice wine
"Puff of Cloud" towlettes; a safety slogan–"one drop of wine for a driver
two streams of tears for a wife"; the mouth of a kettle spout

designed to look like a half-open pair of kissable, cherry-red lips

And there's the cover flap of a purse closed by finely-rendered clasps
depicting the five sense organs; also a building along Chang'an Ave

called "Big Boxer Shorts"[1] by people of Beijing, which describes
its appearance; they also say "the butt's in charge of the brain"
which sums up a certain country's cringe-worthy politics

Now even moist towelettes have dreams of being poetic
The two-kilometer stretch of the Champs-Elysees [1] in Paris
is a clamorous gantlet lined with blandishments and come-ons

Yet who would argue that Chinese New Year and Christmas
are not on a par for the vividness of their poetic pageantry, which also
holds true of inkbrush vs. oil paints, or Western vs. Chinese chess

The usefulness of poetry being expedient [3] is projected in front of us
in all its profuse and pied glory. Sometimes it is in words
sometimes it is a gift that sneaks up in unguarded moments

[1] The CCTV Headquarters was designed by Rem Koolhaas. It consists of
paired highrises linked by a corner-shaped horizontal structure, resembling two
thights joined at the crotch. Originally it was planned as an accessory building for an
even taller structure—the Beijing Television Cultural Center, which had been built
on an adjacent lot. On the eve of the formal opening ceremony for both buildings,
a fireworks accident set the latter structure on fire, and it was destroyed. Only the
"Big Boxer Shorts" building now stands at the site.

[2] The street name "Champs-Elysees" is transliterated in Chinese as *Xiangxie-
lishe* 香榭麗舍, which literaly means "fragrant galleries and lovely lodges." This bears
out the poet's point about the pervasiveness of the poetic impulse: aside from
approximating the sound of the French street name, the Chinese name also conveys
the feel of an exotic street crammed with attractions.

[3] Here the poet puts a twist on a parable of the Taoist thinker Chuang-tzu,
who praised a tree for having unusable wood. Its uselessness enabled it to live long
enough to grow to a giant size, so that people could take shelter under it. Thus
Chuang-tzu believed it ended up an admirable example of "the usefulness of being
useless." The poet echoes this saying, but his examples of "being useful" raise
intriguing questions of what utility is.

12. The reason I have great affliction is that I have a body

--- (Lao Tzu)

L. My Body as Great Affliction or Great Beauty

The world lacks for nothing, yet we feel empty inside
Spring's radiance has not come to dwell in our bodies
and we do not know who we are

I have an orifice to take things in, and another opening
for elimination; I have a functioning body and a simple dwelling
with plain meals, coarse tea, handfuls of pills, and my name

I imagine becoming an eagle that rides the wind, I imagine
a flower offering sips of dew, and my lips warmly smiling
in gratitude to the earth, but these things are not to be

1. My Past Incarnation Was a Sickly Spermatozoa

My past incarnation was a sickly spermatozoa
Before my birth my father was already disabled
My only legacy was a portion of original sin

My Petri dish: Mother, maternal uncle, husband of maternal aunt
one minor intellectual, one right-leaning expert, one suitable candidate
for a public-private partnership, all their lives they didn't make noise

My main nutrient mixture: Great Leap Forward, Anti-Rightist Campaign
Three-Year Famine, and ten troubled years of the Cultural Revolution
In the name of great deeds, I was a locust scourging the countryside

Pupils dilated in eyes glaring green from hunger
I was in fear of everyone, I had contempt for everyone
even in nocturnal emissions I kept abusing lovely females

With no chance to study, I'd have entered my own prison
or gone off to a bandit hideout, into a maw engorged
with the once-decent inhabitants it had gulped down

I was beyond getting tipsy on small amounts of liquor, beyond
being softened by little gestures of amnesty. My smile hid a knife
my delicate, uncallused hand could sting like a poison arrow

13. You who write,

choose a subject suitable to your abilities

--- (Horace, "Ars Poetica")

M. Turning over the Cards of Fate

When we see the word "subject" we see a story
Teasing the thread of "events," we see our lives
nebulous lives, or pale and panicked lives

Certain veins of content are laid out by fate, and thus
one may be touched by one's own or by another's writing
Fate's size is none other than our own size

Writing other things won't count as making an effort at this
We've already done other kinds of writing, industrious or not
more of that would be futile, unless the aim is mere proficiency

m. Slanting Light in a Hospital Room

By then, nothing remained of the friend but embittered hours
on a medical chart; his bed in a cramped spot behind the door
We two sat wordlessly for a long time, he sent me downstairs

Two weeks later I sent him to a courtyard that had a smokestack

Two weeks after that I fell ill and bedridden; a nurse drew back
the drapes, and slanting rays came pouring into the sickroom

I thought, there had never been a time when I wasn't a patient
At home I took care of my gnawing appetite, my sexual desires
When feeling happy I was a fool, when suffering I was a poet

With teacher's cane in hand I stirred the mix of nutrients and poison
which is knowledge, to pour down throats of students, in exchange
for rice, fuel, oil and salt, plus a deep sense of unworthiness

So very common, yet it was heart-wrenching
I think of the harm I did to others, on purpose or not
if they were not fellow patients they were loved ones

In the face of fate, aside from not measuring up
I am rebellious yet at times remorseful, and you will hear
the screech of brakes, the vroom of acceleration

14. The spellbound heart has made
and remade the necklace of songs

---(Tagore, "Unending Love")

N. Humankind's Most Valuable Creation

To encircle a whole city, it takes love
To encircle all of planet earth, only love will do
This is what I've seen, I've undergone

what I'm out to create, only air and water are comparable
Its nakedly exposed treasures are visible anywhere, common
universal, what Jesus spoke of as "omnipresent," moreso than

cars, computers, guided missiles, more than spaceships
more than the steel flowers from thousands of years of science
and artificial bacteria put together by nano-technology

n. Put Love into Action

Without any prior sign, a sinkhole opened in the street
The city has imperceptibly subsided a few centimeters
walls have cracks like silent sobbing grimaces; a future quake

hides its huge spectre; the problem of forced demolitions, the poison
in Sanlu Milk Powder; all stirred up by money, which makes me so uneasy

I almost bark like a dog; may I learn from that loyal creature

that puts love into practice; may I practice relaxing my facial features
My fellow countrymen, don't put on grave looks as if to be impervious
Though my frequent emphasis on this brings ridicule from colleagues

Let me hook love up to other people's hearts, to avoid ischemia
tachycardia, and clotting. Hook it into enterprises and agencies
maybe the work unit will begin to look half human

A loving person is beauty from the inside out, even though
lack of power and money is scorned. A government that doesn't
let love circulate like currency should go on vacation every day

Close the Crowd Control Office, cut down on taxes
cut back on police, auxiliaries and doomsayers of pollution
Let wages ride the up escalator and prices ride the down escalator

15. The Chinese Nation Is at Its Time of Greatest Danger

--- (Tian Han, "March of Volunteer Warriors"
--China's national anthem)

O. The Suspended Sword

In the most telling verse line of the past 100 years
a nation is boiled down to the pivotal line of a poem
"A nation is at its time of greatest danger"

"...Its time of greatest danger" is not about 1911
it is not 1937 or 1946; it is not 1989
It is today, this very day in front of our faces [1]

It is in the downfall of belief, the disarray of morals
Even if a genius could create a brand new way of writing
his precious fabric of words would only be taken for ravings

[1] The year 1911 was when the Qing Dynasty fell to the Nationalists (Kuomintang). The year 1937 was the year that Japan invaded China, beginning the War of Resistance (1937-1045); 1946 was when the civil war between Nationalists and Communists was openly declared; 1989 was when the government suppressed student demonstrations in Tiananment Square and in other large cities.

o. My Prayer

Suppose a nation's top intellects were struck by successive pathologies

brains cobwebbed, degraded and debased, telling lies without restraint
then a nationality would be at its time of greatest danger

Suppose businessmen stooped to new levels of greed and stupidity
trying to write their own names on every bill of paper money
then a nationality would be at its time of greatest danger

Suppose the people considered belonging to the people shameful
like ants in knotholes that no longer thought of working
then a nationality would be at its time of greatest danger

Suppose rivers in the grip of gunky scum let out screams
like in Monck's picture, and fresh breezes pretended not to look
suppose a host of genes were altered, and budding life

was sapped of zest, then a nationality would be at its time
of greatest danger; language would be a series of gasps
rhymes would be garbage, queasily looping and oozing

Good sir! Were you aware of this many years ago
and so wrote that grieving line to be etched on our bones?
Good sir! What shall we do to lay your mind at rest?

16. In This Era, What Is a Poet For

--- (Heidegger)

P. Writing Poetry and Writing the History of Poetry

What is a poet's purpose? Of course he has to write poetry
to write poems on letter-size paper, on his thighs
then nonchalantly follow that pair of thighs into the history of poetry

All the way he runs after those beautiful feet, with all he's got
from metaphors to refusing metaphors, then to
the lower body school, then adding a lot of narrative elements

Narrate trivial things until they become unbearable
then write about culture until it's unrelated to culture
Write poetry's history to the point of forgetting poetry

p. In a Visual Age, Give Attention to Voices

Close your eyes awhile, remember cassette tapes in damp boxes
and scratched up vinyl records. A woodsman's resounding axe-blows
have become vanishing notes, due to laws protecting forests

A millstone once turned to the rhythm of donkeys' hoofs
We who wished to keep the ancients near us could only tug

at their clothes, but their sleeves tore like whisked-away clouds

Lovers who once coupled in the wilds now call for a hotel room
We hear harvesters rumbling; wheat plants get their fill of chemicals
now that rapid growth is a route to the city for plump kernels

Gas stations and toll booths are closely spaced; physiques of singers
are puffed up, and lip synching has a factory's worth of stage effects
A neighbor girl after plastic surgery appears outside your condo block

In primary school you can hear students reading aloud; in middle school
there's nothing to listen to, except the sound of institutions losing hope
Cover your ears and crawl into a haystack, you'll still hear cries for help

Do re me fa so la si… A money printing machine has diarrhea [1]
and the banks are secretly glad. One, two, three, four, five, six, seven
first the numbers are sung in a song, later they count material desires

[1] The last two syllables of the scale are "la si," which sounds like the Chinese word *la-xi* 拉稀, meaning "diarrhea." Some students cannot resist making wisecracks about this. The money printing machine may be a veiled reference to after school exam prep programs, which are exploited by some teachers and administrators to make extra money.

17. We choose what we will make ourselves to be

--- *(Sartre, "Existentialism Is a Humanism")*

Q. I May Have Encountered Sartre Face-to-Face

Seven years ago in Paris, I passed a small bar several times
where he had once been a regular, and I imagined him there
smoking his pipe, filling a wine glass at a table by the window

Today I walk down a street in Beijing, watching the faces
of yellow-skinned people who hurry by...greeting the ones
I recognize, smiling at the ones I do not know

That's all it takes to make my afternoon nearly beautiful
like a well-earned reward, but also like unlooked for riches
or being in Sartre's company as I measure my steps

q. A Certain Day on My Own

At noon I refused a honey-tongued seller of "fitness supplies"
who was eager to come to my place and offer services
In the afternoon I "forgot" a supposedly important meeting

For 50 minutes I read Si Maqian's history book; for half an hour
watched the news in English; wrote nine album leaves of calligraphy

of which the one in Zheng Xie's style came out best of all

I rested eyes on the carpet of the lawn, made wet by a shower
on a day forecast to be overcast changing to cloudy
At night I had dreams, caused by a few mosquitos

The mosquito coil gave off harsh smoke; I got up and
and wrote an essay titled "The 'Panfeng Conference Was Just
a Blip of Self–Contradiction between Breakfast and Lunch"[1]

"Coal briquets are black" and "Lantern Festival Snowballs are White"
Both of these are true, but they aren't addressed to each other
and neither mentions roundness… Then I went back to sleep

In the morning I went walking, and in the afternoon taught a class
I taught a kind of erudition disconnected from salt and cooking oil
or else I made it my duty to misguide them as best I could

[1] The 'Crossing of Swords at Panfeng' was a series of polemical battles between the "Intellectual Writing" and "Folk Writing" camps of contemporary Chinese poetry. Some of the main figures in the former camp were Cheng Guangwei, Zang Di and Xi Du. Key figures in the latter camp included Yi Sha and Shen Haobo. The dispute came to a head in essays and during conferences held during 1999 in Beijing. Prior to the conferences, many poets assumed the polemics were just a means of livening up the poetry scene, but the heated disputes showed there was not much common ground for nuanced discussion.

18. Cut bamboo, assemble bamboo,
make clay pellets, chase living flesh

--- ("Crossbow Song"---an ancient song of the Spring Autumn Period)

R. Watch the Ancients Go Hunting

In this song we watch a forebear splitting bamboo with raspy strokes
He crafts a bow with rapid tapping, then catapults a whizzing stone
at the sound of the bowstring a bird falls, and a cooking fire is lit

We imagine his sinewy frame dressed in a breechcloth, bare feet running
like the wind, his ruddy face, looking as if he'd stepped from a painting
A song played on a loop is absorbed into poems by someone literate

but the original verse writer never claimed to have poetic talent
Performance art and written words both share something with us
though one has visceral elan, the other is showing a pallor

r. A Girl Named Junna

A girl named Junna from Rizhao City in Shandong
her breeze-stirred locks and sidelong glance stay in your mind
Junna, that girl so serene and even-tempered

Junna who made the rounds from boy to boy

who was glad to date them one after another
She only needed to leaf through books to get an "A"

now treats her mother dutifully, takes good care
of her little sister; she who came back from California
with a degree in film studies—she vowed to perform

kind acts by the thousands for all the folks she knew
and those she didn't; with her devoted heart she wished
to prove that everyone is worth cherishing

"Ah, it was nothing; it only took a tiny effort!"
But with such efforts the world would be different from before
and I would no longer be doubtful of poetry, of beauty

My wife bumped me and asked "Were you in love with her?"
I thought a bit, and answered "yes." We lifted our heads
to the remote summer stars, filled with love's sorrow

19. The world is a stage, but the play is badly cast

--- (Oscar Wilde, "Lord Savile's Crime")

S. Greatness, or That Stale, Old Role

High officials are not great; a general amnesty is not greatness
A master artist doesn't always remember where his home is
Today's great men are like the grasshopper caught

under a straw hat thrown by a child. Obama doesn't count
as a hero, and Assad does not come close
Wolf-eyed Putin is just a president who likes arm wrestling

Greatness is but a wind blowing through the human world; it is
the simple but sensitive heart; the desperate leaf-like hands reaching
to hold back a maddened locomotive, until the last moment

s. Go back to Being Yourself

I don't know if I can still pull open my drapes of curiosity
namely imagination, which is often as low and melancholy
as the pale belly of a swallow in its nest.

I once wrote on paper: be yourself, go back to being yourself
Have these shallow ink traces already been erased?

Go back to being yourself—can I really do that?

Can I show a lucid gaze worthy of a sage's gyrus of wisdom?
Can I grow a young man's bulging biceps once again?
Can I keep my good-heartedness and inborn taciturnity?

Perhaps a different life would be more suited to my nature and talents
When a school teacher called roll, I used to belt out "here"
Now I'm aloof, I let the one who's called be the one to go

Only at the sight of my child do I bend down
My farsighted eyes need only see the word "Mother"
they will still moisten… The person I am at this moment

is but a fragment of my life's duration so far
My handful of poems are like ten uneven fingers
all of them alike will eventually fall into the dust

20. We only enjoy the happiness we are able to understand

--- (Maeterlinck, "The Blue Bird")

T. That Was a Different Time and Place

Once I was whiling away the time on a Santiago Beach
An aircraft carrier from the 7th Fleet once stood quietly offshore
before firing its cannons it was struck by bombs... and I once

ambled at a crossing near the triumphal arch... The stores
were crammed with Chinese who snatched up LV bags
shooting glances at times envious and at times disdainful

In Singapore, where Chinese language is called "Hua-yu" (华语)
at the Gulf of Siam Night Market, beside the fountain
I was sized up by as a carouser and led on provocatively

t. Poetry and Its Era: Descending Scale

I stumble upon a poem, stumble upon a mood, such as
in Nanxun Old Town of Huzhou, at Little Lotus Estate [1]
and many other places in dreams

I look up at the Estate's name on an imposing plaque
going forward, one step leads into the moon

not the moon per se, but through the moon gate

Within it, what sways to the round of seasons?
—a panorama of views that could be at West Lake
not West Lake, just lotuses in the farmstead's pond

raising green canopies like at West Lake, and the pink beauty
of flowers that go with the poetry of Yang Wanli
I am like a Zhou Dynasty folk song collector, chanting

"Lotus leaves spread in fields." I wasn't sent to find songs
I'm a strolling visitor, for reasons having to do with ticket sales
greeted by a breeze the owner Liu Yong [2] summoned

Not Liu Yong per se, but the attractive guide who leads my way
a young woman, discoursing on the wind... not wind per se
but the whirl of hospitality that swept up Liu Yong's guests

[1] Nanxun is a district within Huzhou City, which is located to the south of
Lake Taihu in Zhejiang Province. Little Lotus Estate is a historical park within
Nanxun Old Town.

[2] Liu Yong (1829-1899) was a Huzhou merchant who built the Little Lotus
Farmstead. He was well known for his hospitatlity and his literary gatherings.

21. Each day I reflect three times on my conduct

--- (Zengzi, Analects)

U. Amid a Flurry of Italic Letters

Wind blows slantwise, rainfall is slantwise, as are hands
jammed arrogantly in pockets. The leader's face on a flawed coin
looks crooked. Slanted too are the signatures of big shot stars

in lines like whirling dragons. Models fawned over by spotlights walk
down a catwalk with crossover steps, to win applause that sounds
like a pan of sizzling kidneys. Their moves prey on your mind

Even the smeared sunset is not content with going straight down
I expand my chest, draw the breath deeper; each day I reflect
thrice on my conduct, within half an hour of mealtimes

u. Write Down Our Crimes against Language

For he who turned himself in, the outcome of taking the right path
may be hard to face. Around him survival is still temporizing
recklessly swiping a card at self-checkout, wanting to believe

the fish grew up in a stream, where countless Manchurian cranes
were gathered. The arm of poetry is dislocated at the shoulder

she can not keep reality's top-heavy brain erect

The people are urged to grow fat, fatigue and unease pack the belly
the gut gas-distended, the prostate inflamed, and so on. But the people
are not so obese they will stay afloat despite their inability to swim

Time is cashed in for small change, into nickel-and-dime faces
nickels and dimes jostling together, you are resentful of me, and I
hold you in contempt, all our lives mouthing words not worth a fart

Only self-esteem chastises me for what I say, makes me want to cry
only self-esteem is like a clearing cloth that is still not too grimy
should we use it to make a flag or a pair of underpants?

Our crimes against language cannot be forgiven lightly
Even our forebears knew the importance of concealing shame
We cannot have everyone going naked, running after a flag

22. Be less curious about people

and more curious about ideas

--- *(Madame Curie)*

V. Children Rehearse for the Adult World

My five-year-old plays with building blocks, and beside them
stands yesterday's handiwork, graced with small red flowers
he is fully absorbed, putting together a little house

saying to himself: "Lu Shengde is best at piling blocks"
then sticks a self-congratulatory flower in his chest pocket
actually the one he made yesterday is prettier than today's

Today he didn't make a nice one, but he needs a reward
and how are we adults any different, setting our own rules?
We never tire of commending and making much of ourselves

v. Rules and Standards

This is not the only laughable thing about adults
They take themself as the measuring stick for all things
for instance an elephant is big, compared to our stature

For instance, drawing comparisons between one's own thigh

and someone else's arm, or Shakyamuni vs. Apostle John
or hold an uncontested match naming the black-haired one

to be winner, or someone who just knows the English word
"Yes." So called friends or enemies are the ones
who conspire for one's vital interests or stand against them

Two thirds of national leaders I see have been infected
by pernicious moral disease, and the look on a moralist's face
give cause for suspicion. Humanity grows like rampant weed

without conferring much value or meaning on this planet
An honor for members of one group is poison for another
yet they expect to remain calm and undisturbed

My name is a simple signifier, just a few strokes slanting
right or left; my forehead wishes for life to be writ large
but my cringing tail drags it into smallness

23\. My aspiration was to become a minor poet,
and I've succeeded.

--- (Borges)

W. Even Borges Was This Way

We poets are all minor figures
By adding 'us' together we get
one incomplete great poet. As for Borges

he has already arrived, we are on the road
Amid vicissitudes of desire we obey time's commands
and are blessed with a livelihood the size of a fingernail

It is an honor on the scale of a mole on the skin
It is an honor in the time frame of a malignancy
It is an honor such as we have never attained

w. Once I Considered It But Could Not Do It; Still I Consider It

Once I thought, let me be a poet of imposing fame
like Heine was in his day: "If you say the name
most worthy of renown, you will say my name"

Once I thought, poetry already encompasses everything
I need not trouble myself to make a lame continuation
but I heard strains of music in my heart saying, "Wrong"

Once I thought, I'll write one thousand good poems
and submit them under one thousand assumed names
The journals containing the poems would be sent out

but returned to sender, and the reason given would be—
"Recipient Unknown." On one hand I keep my day job
on the other I travel the world, like Whitman who did not

overlook any corner, giving kindness and beauty their due
however unimposing. Stroke by stroke I patiently depict them
chanting softly so as not to disturb the slightest chirp

On one hand I write, on the other I feel moved, for such beauty
however unimposing, is the supreme creation of humble souls
In this world we only find poems, not poets

24. Plucking mums beneath the eastern hedge,
I serenely gaze at mountains to the south

--- *(Tao Yuanming)*

X. Chrysanthemums and Their Root Systems

A chrysanthemum's root system is how charisma looks in the Orient
A wisp of scent transports me to back to the Tang, back to
the breath of Jin. Exquisite mum, its profuse petals counterposed

and its fragrance spreading far, outdoes the voluptuous, worldly peony
Mum, flower of self-esteem, bud of gentility, though rocked by wind
against each other, never stints from spreading trust and good intent

I want to devote an entire chapter of literary history to Tao Qian,
reciting 'Peach Blossom Spring' beside Wangfujing Street
to be heard by all plant life and human life under heaven

x. Nature in a Concrete Forest

A friend has moved to the suburbs, to float like a cloud
white and ethereal. Who has dreams that don"t include
a bright, clear sky? Who doesn't want to smooth out wrinkles?

My friend is a professor of classical aesthetics, his new place

an elegant frame house of Russian design, with folksy Hunan decor
I joked it's like wearing a dirndl top under a tailored suit

How many rooms? As Tao Yuanming foretold, "eight or nine rooms."
There's a security monitor in the living room aimed at a money tree
in the yard, but certainly no "rooster crowing on a mulberry branch"

Eggplants, peppers and lots of green veggies grow in the yard
Grass was dug up to plant "beans and sprouts," enough to stay home
ten days at a time, to spend easeful hours in a cement forest

There is nowhere to hang my present, a "Mountain Hermit" painting
so I take it home, just as there's no place for it in my noisy heart
Since I forgive myself, I might as well forgive my friend

which reminds me, only while writing poetry do I remember
what Confucian virtues mean. Time after time I betrayed
my own trust; I wore opera masks to go outdoors

25. You will not stumble if you choose the path

--- (Egypt, The Book of Going forth by Day)

Y. Science Is Trial and Error, So Is Human Life

I once stumbled face down, repelled by a certain notion
It was one impulse, two wisps of emotion and three words
an unspoken remark and a half-baked metaphor, seemingly fresh

yet it drew blood. That innocent act felt like a crime
The ambiguity of a single sentence–almost betrayed me
with traps of imagery and teetering discursive structure

All my artistic creations, currents of thought, ideal conceptions
were borrowed from my companions, even the lethe-waters of fame
Now I break out sweating, back then it seemed like an OK plan

y. The Road of the Crowd, A Road for Oneself

The rabbit running with youthful speed young does not ridicule
my current turtle steps. My pace has turned sluggish
My lines of poetry use more and more punctuation marks

My nether parts lack stamina, morning erections are fewer than ever
this is a personal secret I do not like to mention; and as for

what I'm living through, to say it's a grim struggle is not far off

After 40 minutes of exercise at dusk, I rely on white hair
to push on with my night reading. My lenses
and inspirations flash fleetingly like pangs of illness

For 30 years I have pushed toward my own goals
I steel myself to keep going; I adjust goals and direction
my path made by treading takes me ever further from others

All of my hatred has been discarded, and envious pangs
are like rice at the bottom of a crock during a famine
again and again they reappear, each time a little weaker

It hasn't been easy washing my foulness
A man on the road does not forget his dear brothers
I give them blessings, and do not forget myself

26. ...and miles to go before I sleep

and miles to go before I sleep

---(Robert Frost)

Z. Robert Frost, a Poet of Perception, Emotion and Gratitude

The Robert Frost who was a country doctor
who measured country roads beneath his feet
got his finger on the pulse of living. To utter it

he returned to the root of things, drew near their truths
I seem to keep him company, pacing along field borders
craning my neck at starry reaches so supremely vast

For lowly humans and himself he wrote poetic stanzas
softly offering canticles to ripe smells and heaven's favor
in daily observances, as he passed through the ribcage of time

z. Compline Prayer

At this moment, sounds of commotion gradually fade
from air as quiet as night-blooming flowers; beside my ear
a voice says the time is right for writing poems

A voice says the time is right for a chanted prayer
I have given up my all-knowing angle of vision
and taken initiative to restore the rhythm of daily life

to restore its slowness, to go hand in hand with written words
through springtime that won't turn about for cries of the countryside
while living in the world makes me a heap of scrap metal

or into a clod of moist earth, with my face turned toward Dante
which will only lead me to despair from head to toe
We are a bunch of resplendent minor poets,

a pack of wordsmiths ashamed to be called poets
we face heaven's vault, and our earthward aspect
registers the precarity of this dusty world,

Where inconsequential verses gather we swap manuscripts
A tide surges in our hearts, even as we harbor secret hurt
and autumn's slight chill congeals in tears on our faces

January-September 2012, Beijing

ESSAYS

Lu Jian's Inner Journey in Poetry

By Shan Zhansheng

Since the 1980s, China's modern poetry scene has seen the emergence of numerous currents and schools of thought, as well as self-proclaimed or recognized poetic groups. These include the "Misty School," "New Realism," "They," "Non-Nonism," "Ruffians," "Old Summer Palace Group," "Divine Writing," "New Rural Poetry," "Intellectual Writing," "Folk Writing," "Third Way Writing," "Lower Body Poetry," and "Middle Generation Poetry," along with numerous other local groups. If we were to search within these groups for Lu Jian's name, it would be difficult to find him. However, Lu Jian and his poetry's influence have been a real presence since the 1980s. At a seminar on Lu Jian's poetry, poet Ye Yanbin noted, "Lu Jian's poetry is a phenomenon worthy of study, for he is a relatively unique poet in contemporary poetry. He has been writing poetry for 30 years, maintaining his own unique creative identity amidst numerous trends and schools... While the leading figures in each trend gradually fade away, Lu Jian still holds his own." Ye Yanbin made these remarks on the morning of May 10, 2007. Five years later, his assessment of Lu Jian remains accurate and insightful. Lu's new collection of poetry, *Songs of a Resplendent Minor Poet*, presented to the poetry scene five years later, further reinforces the value and significance of Ye Yanbin's words.

In fact, research on Lu Jian's poetry has been ongoing for decades. As far as I know, the earliest critical review was Liu Shilin's appreciation of Lu Jian's poetry, followed by a comprehensive evaluation of his early works, titled "The Power of Man, the Vision of the Heart." After the publication of Lu Jian's masterpiece *Famous Cities and Gates*, the renowned poetry critic Shen Qi wrote a particularly valuable article on Lu Jian titled

"Poetic City's Unique Door." This review not only evaluated the collection but also Lu Jian's poetry. Another insightful poetry critic, Yang Jizhe, devoted a lengthy essay titled "On Lu Jian's Long Poems." This comprehensive study of Lu Jian's long poem series "The Geneva Sun," which "takes foreign historical figures and events as its subject matter," argues that Lu Jian not only "drags us into the depths of time, into the arena of material power and awareness of life, allowing us to witness an unprecedented drama," but also demonstrates his "outstanding narrative ability." Later, after the publication of Lu Jian's four books of documentary poetry, the Communication University of China held a symposium on his poetry in 2007. The resulting transcript (see the May 2007 issue of *Literary Gazette*) concluded that "he is a 'poetic phenomenon' worthy of study." At the conference, poets, critics, and professors including Tu An, Ye Yanbin, Li Xiaoyu, Tang Xiaodu, Zhou Yueliang, Wang Yansheng, Lin Mang, Zhang Qinghua, Zhu Xianshu, He Xiaobing, and Xu Gang all expressed their unique perspectives on Lu Jian's poetry, declaring him an "an irreplaceable poet." As far as I know, there are far more articles evaluating Lu Jian's poetry than these (some of which can be found in the 172,000-word article collection on Lu Jian's poetry, *About a Poet*, published by Baihua Literature and Art Publishing House in February 1997). Here I am reviewing the evaluations of Lu Jian's poetry by critics from different periods, simply to raise the question: What kind of "phenomenon" is Lu Jian, as a "phenomenon"?

"A school unto his own in the city of poetry," "an irreplaceable poet," "a poetic phenomenon worthy of study"—these descriptions, uttered by poets and critics Shen Qi, Kuang Man, and Ye Yanbin, represent a shared understanding of Lu Jian among many poets and critics. So, what is the uniqueness of Lu Jian's emergence as a "phenomenon" in Chinese poetry over the past thirty years, and what is its value and significance for research? Here, I would like to express my understanding by quoting a line from Li Li's essay "Saving Poetry and Saving the World: The Motivation and Value of Lu Jian's Poetry" (published in the July 2012 edition of *Shilin* magazine). He stated, "Lu

Jian's greatest contribution is to offer us a new possibility for writing outside the traditional aesthetic categories of poetry." Li Li's statement refers to the four books of documentary poetry Lu Jian has written since 2003. In fact, a general review of Lu Jian's poetic career reveals that he consistently creates poetry outside the prevailing aesthetic categories of the poetry world in which he works. Standing outside the current, exploring new possibilities for poetic aesthetics has always been a hallmark of Lu Jian's subjective consciousness and practical behavior in his poetry creation. If we take a simplified approach and divide Lu Jian's poetry over the past thirty years into four sections, we can more clearly see the mental journey and aesthetic changes in Lu Jian's poetry creation, and more effectively understand the characteristics and value significance of Lu Jian's poetry creation.

Lu Jian's poetry career began in the early 1980s, when the dominant trend in the poetry world was the poetic movement called "Misty Poetry," also known as the "New Tide." It's fair to say that all poets in the contemporary poetry world were influenced and impacted by Misty Poetry. Its influence on Lu Jian was also evident. Unlike many poets who simply followed the Misty Poetry trend, Lu Jian, while influenced by it, also took new steps forward based on it. The impact of Misty Poetry on the poetry world of the time can be examined from two perspectives. First, its influence on social and human perceptions. Second, its influence on poetic, artistic methods and forms. Regarding its impact on social perceptions, its primary achievement was its harsh political critique of the extreme leftist ideology of the Cultural Revolution and its aftermath. Regarding its impact on human perceptions, its primary achievement was its powerful promotion of the "human" writ large and its dignified expression of human dignity through its poetry and poetic theory. In terms of artistic influence, Misty Poetry, with its subtle modernist characteristics, completely revolutionized the art of poetry compared to the three decades after the founding of the People's Republic of China. It can be said that Misty Poetry's influence on Chinese poetry was profound, extensive, and lasting. Lu Jian, whose rise to prominence under the profound influence of Misty Poetry, also explored the depths of human nature and the forefront of art under its influence. If Misty Poetry's exploration of social and human issues reinforced the richness of human nature, Lu Jian's poetry illuminated the complexity of society and life. Without even looking through Lu Jian's collections from that period, I clearly remember a short poem from that period titled "Beauty, Innocence, Kindness, and Tragedy." The poem describes the beauty of flowers and butterflies, the freedom of flowers and the freedom of butterflies. When flowers and butterflies exist independently, their beauty, freedom, and freedom are all real. Yet, tragedy occurs precisely in the close proximity of these two kinds of beauty. When a butterfly flutters into the embrace of a beautiful flower, when the beautiful flower embraces the beautiful butterfly with its own beautiful passion, the flower's poisonous pollen kills the butterfly, and the butterfly's scent withers the flower. While exploring the complexities of human nature and society, Lu Jian, in his poetic art, departs from the lingering sentimentality of Misty Poetry, and from the rhetorical devices often employed in Misty Poetry, which alternate between symbolism and metaphor, to a direct description of the subject. This direct description, within the framework of the poem, takes on a metaphorical dimension, giving his poetry a pioneering, robust style. At this point, Lu Jian's poetry seems to have a hard shell, but within this shell lies Lu Jian's rational reflections on society and life. In a sense, from the outset, Lu Jian has positioned his poetry on the basis of "intellectual" writing. Perhaps it is precisely because of this premise that his poetry, like him, always conveys a sense of sharp, hard-edged toughness. Time passes silently, and many things pass by in the blink of an eye. When we look back at the past, we always seem to discover many things that are self-evident. For example, if we examine Lu Jian's poetic style at that time from today's perspective, we will naturally find that the ongoing changes and continuities of Lu Jian's poetry in theme and style serve to illustrate Lu Jian's efforts to break away quickly from the influence of Misty Poetry and pursue his own independent poetic stance.

From Lu Jian's successful escape from the influence of Misty Poetry to his work "Songs of a Resplendent Minor Poet," his poetry has twice transcended and broken away from his earlier poetic style. The reality of Chinese poetry in recent decades demonstrates that while it's not difficult for a talented poet to break away from and transcend the influence of current trends, it's certainly more difficult to break away from and transcend one's existing style while maintaining one's own poetic perspectives and stances. Lu Jian has achieved this, I believe. This is perhaps why Ye Yanbin considers Lu Jian a poetic phenomenon worthy of study. More importantly, while Lu Jian was breaking away from and transcending himself, both of these creative transformations laid a solid foundation for "Songs of a Resplendent Minor Poet." When we examine Lu Jian's poetic journey in the context of the recent three decades of Chinese poetry, we can better appreciate the importance and value of Lu Jian's creative work, grounded in his own poetic stance and perspectives. For Chinese poets of the past three decades, there seems to be a curse that's difficult to escape. This curse is the poetry world's repeated subversive writing as practiced up to now. This repetitive subversion has perpetuated the pattern of extreme leftist ideological writing in Chinese poetry, while simultaneously ignoring the cultural traditions and poetic consciousness of modern Chinese poetry since its inception. This has transformed subversion into a mere pursuit of subversion itself. From the moment Lu Jian entered the poetry world, he never incorporated subversive writing into his own oeuvre. Standing outside of successive poetic trends and schools, he passionately pursued his own creations. I don't intend to criticize subversive writing here. In a sense, I fully affirm it. However, I would also like to point out that modern Chinese poetry, from its inception, has shouldered the dual mission of both subversion and construction. In the early days of modern poetry, many believed it was merely a matter of destroying old forms and creating new ones. However, after the spread of Symbolist poetry in modern Chinese poetry, people gradually realized that for modern Chinese poetry, the subversion or "revolution" involved more than just the old poetic forms; more importantly, it involved a revolutionary overthrow of one's own mindset. Therefore, "revolution" and "subversion" naturally became both a latent and overt driving force in the development of modern Chinese poetry. Whether turning "westward" or "eastward," this drive accompanies poets like a shadow. Since the 1980s, using subversion as a driving force for writing has not only become a common phenomenon in the poetry world, but one could even argue that many poets consider this "subversive" writing a "poetic path," a "royal path" that can catapult them to fame through "subversion." Thus, the original poetic significance of "revolution" and "subversion" in modern Chinese poetry has been "alienated" and utterly corrupted through its repeated practice as the "royal path." Frankly, for someone long immersed in the poetic landscape and facing such a reality, maintaining independence and self-sufficiency is no easy task, no matter what approach one adopts.

Lu Jian's true artistic self-awareness began in the early 1990s. The publication of his two poetry collections, *Famous Cities and Gates* and *The Geneva Sun*, exemplifies this clear and conscious awareness of his poetic independence. *Famous Cities and Gates* (published by Culture and Art Publishing House in September 1992), comprises sixty-six poems, both independent and interconnected, that form a vast historical space. The poetic elements that compose this vast historical space are Lu Jian's narratives of forty-eight modern and contemporary Chinese cultural figures and masters, a dialogue between the poet and these forty-eight contemporary Chinese culture bearers. Of particular note is the way Lu Jian places these forty-eight contemporary Chinese cultural figures, or forty-eight culture bearers, within the poetic spaces separated by thirteen poems titled "Gates." Thus, this collection of poems constitutes both a vast city-state space and the poet's vast spiritual space. Published concurrently with *Famous Cities and Gates*, Lu Jian's other poetry collection, *The Geneva Sun* (published by Taiwan Shizhihua Publishing House in October 1992), consists of seven long poems depicting prominent figures in Western history and culture. These include Queen Elizabeth II, Archimedes, Alexander, Albert Einstein, D.H. Lawrence and Frida Kahlo,

Van Gogh, and Calvin. Renowned critics Shen Qi and Yang Jizhe have each offered insightful evaluations of these two collections. In his lengthy essay on Lu Jian's collection *Famous Cities and Gates*, Shen Qi calls Lu Jian's poetry "a school unto itself in the city of poetry," saying that Lu Jian "has opened for us a unique and extraordinary door to existence." Shen Qi not only examines the historical space revealed by the unique subject matter, the symphonic epic momentum presented by the unique structure, and the poetic tension generated by the unique language, but more importantly, he addresses the question of Lu Jian's uniqueness in the poetry world of his time, as raised at the beginning of his essay. Although Shen Qi didn't delve deeper into this issue at the time, today, his ability to address it reinforces his unique vision and profound understanding of the poetry world. In Shen Qi's view, as the dust settles on each poetic wave, as we "reflect, sort out, and integrate" the historical experience of poetry, we should no longer "ignore" those poets we have "repeatedly neglected," those who "calmly drifted" outside the current, "deeply engaging with the entire modernist new poetry movement while maintaining an independent poetic and transcendental perspective, focusing on and studying the works and personalities of marginal poets." Sixteen years have passed since Shen Qi articulated this perspective. Now, when we reflect on Lu Jian through the lens of Shen Qi's perspective, we can better appreciate his clarity and insight, and even more so, Lu Jian's value to the poetry world at that time.

It's important to point out that the issue we're discussing today extends beyond Shen Qi's aforementioned assertions and understandings. We intend to examine the dimensions of Lu Jian's spiritual time and space through his two poetry collections, *Famous Cities and Gates* and *The Geneva Sun*. Indeed, the independent poetic spirit and personality traits that have characterized Lu Jian's work from its inception to the present day are universally acknowledged. Our exploration of the dimensions and evolution of Lu Jian's spiritual space in poetry today aims to raise the question of the spiritual structure of Chinese new poets, using Lu Jian as a case study. I personally believe that, after a long period of striving for self-expressive poetic creation, raising this question will have significant implications for the long-term development of Chinese poetry. Furthermore, by examining the spiritual space of Lu Jian, as revealed in these two poetry collections, we can more clearly discern the underlying connections that led to the respective choices he made in his earlier and later works.

As mentioned earlier, in his work *Famous Cities and Gates*, Lu Jian constructs a three-dimensional spiritual fortress of modern and contemporary Chinese culture. In *The Geneva Sun*, Lu Jian, through his poetic reflections on Western sages, builds a shared spiritual sky for humanity and offers a profound reflection on the darkness inherent in this clarity. It is important to note that in reflecting on the thoughts and actions of Western sages, Lu Jian not only draws on a profound and profound Eastern cultural perspective, but also examines them from a metaphysical perspective of human thought and action that transcends race and region. This reflection incorporates both empirical reflections on human life and a transcendental perspective. Critic Yang Jizhe has offered a unique and insightful assessment of several of the long poems in *The Geneva Sun*. He said, "Lu Jian pondered and questioned many aspects of human life: war, peace, religion, sex, art, and prevalent social ills. These are all presented and unfolded in his writings, tending towards a profound and thorough understanding, embodying the heights of wisdom attained through long periods of human practice and painstaking reflection." (Yang Jizhe, "On Lu Jian's Long Poems") *Regarding Famous Cities and Gates* and *The Sun of Geneva*, Shen Qi and Yang Jizhe's interpretations and evaluations are insightful and insightful. I repeatedly recommend Shen Qi and Yang Jizhe's assessments of Lu Jian's poetry because they both truly recognize the unusual poetic elements in Lu Jian's poetry. This unusual poetic element is the poetic space-time that transcends time, presented in Lu Jian's poetry. We should truly recognize that Lu Jian's excursion into space-time during this period was a unique phenomenon in the Chinese poetry world of that era. Lu Jian's spiritual excursion at this time not only established his own independent and self-sufficient poetic concept, but also injected a new atmosphere into the domestic poetry scene at that time, expanding the spiritual space-time of Chinese poetry to a greater extent. Subsequently, Lu Jian also entered a phase of unfettered creation because of this excursion.

If Lu Jian's *Famous Cities and Gates* and *The Geneva Sun* fulfilled his ideal of a poetic excursion into the empyrean, then the publication of *Warmth* (Liaoning People's Publishing House, December 2008) marked a new phase in his creative career. *Warmth* brings together four collections of poetry written between 2004 and 2007: "34 Gifts," "Tianlou, Tianlou," "Bill on the Maple Leaf," and "Sunshine of the Luo River." These four collections capture the details of Lu Jian's life. "Sunshine of the Luo River" explores his hometown and his friends, the foundation of his life and the roots of his soul; "Bill on the Maple Leaf" depicts his son, his famil ties; "Tianlou, Tianlou" represents his journey from his hometown into society, his encounter with the earth; and "34 Gifts" depicts his dialogues with his students, a metaphor for his interplay with society. Hometown, family, society; family members, neighbors, classmates, fellow villagers, teachers, relatives, friends, parents, and students—his connections with these people, or rather, these people's connections with him, reveal the texture of his life and illuminate his life experiences. In fact, it's not just these subjects—not what he wrote or how he wrote them—that should be further emphasized. Rather, it's the shift from the historical time and space of *Famous Cities and Gates* and *The Geneva Sun* to the present time and space, and the significance and value this shift reveals for his work. From poetic wanderings of the soul to the tangible experiences of the people and events around him, from soaring imagination to plain narrative, Lu Jian achieved a shift from the sky to the earth, imbuing his poetry with a historical depth imbued with boundless tension. This shift—from the vastness of historical time and space to the concrete, detailed reality of time and space, from the lofty sages and wise men of the heavens to the ordinary people living and surviving alongside the poet, from unbridled imagination to authentic, direct expression— enabled   him   to   expand   his   poetic   thinking   and   technique comprehensively, laying a solid foundation for his later work. From then on, his creative freedom was fully realized.

In the following, let us begin our interpretation of *Songs of a Resplendent Minor Poet*. In a sense, the periodized description of Lu Jian's poetry given above, seems not simply to interpret Lu Jian at its previous stage, but rather to point from that time and place here and now. This reminds me of the "Four Paths" of Buddhist practice. According to the *Encyclopedia of Chinese Buddhism*, the "Four Paths" refer to the four stages of Buddhist practice leading to the elimination of afflictions, the realization of truth, and entering nirvana, namely—the path of preparation, the non-stinting path the path of liberation, and the path of superior progress. The path of preparation, also known as the expedient path, is the preparatory practice for the elimination of afflictions; the non-stinting path, also known as the path of no hindrance, is the stage where practitioners directly eliminate afflictions; the path of liberation is the stage after the non-stinting path, when a single thought of wisdom arises, leading to realization of truth and liberation from afflictions; and the path of superior progress, also known as the path of victory, which is the period of increasing concentration and wisdom after liberation. This author does not intend to draw a rigid parallel between the "Four Paths" of Buddhist practice and the various stages of Lu Jian's creative process. I simply find many similarities between the four paths of Buddhist practice and Lu Jian's poetic creation. Wang Guowei, in his *Talks on Lyric Poetry of the Human Realm* also discussed the "three realms" of life and poetry. He believed that those who aspire to great things in life must pass through these three realms: the first, "Last night, the west wind withered the green trees; I climbed the high tower alone, gazing out at the endless horizon"; the second, "My belt is growing looser, yet I never regret; I am worn out pining for that person"; the third, "I have searched a thousand times among the crowds, but suddenly turning about, I see her standing in the dim light." Wang Guowei was discussing life, but because he used poetry to describe it, later generations have come to recognize these as the three realms of poetic creation. In reality, life and poetry are the same. Achieving anything seems to involve a process. Ultimately, it all comes down to the outcome. Only by achieving the true fruit, realizing the truth, and seeing "that person" can we see the extraordinary significance and value inherent in this process; only thus can we truly appreciate the indispensability of each link in this process, and discern the connection between the spiritual space-time carried by the most recent link in this chain. Perhaps this is what we often call hindsight. Here, too, as a wise man with hindsight, we examine *Songs of a Resplendent Minor Poet* again. We can see that Lu Jian's work at this point has reached a state of unimpeded creative freedom, and his work simultaneously carries all the information from his previous poetic and spiritual space-time. If we approach this issue from a different perspective, we can also see that Lu Jian's current poetry derives precisely from the profound and extensive accumulation of his previous works, which makes it possible for him to enter this realm of creative freedom.

So, what does "Songs of a Magnificent Little Poet" offer us? I believe the following points warrant our attention.

First, the ritualistic nature of his poetic construct.

Songs of a Resplendent Minor Poet is both a collection of poems and a poem cycle with a coherent and ingenious structure. Perhaps it is precisely this collection that has intensified my interest in the ritualistic nature of Lu Jian's poetic form. *Songs of a Resplendent Minor Poet*" comprises 26 cantos, or strictly speaking, 26 pairs of poems. Each pair is led by an overarching title, numbered in Arabic numerals. Under this overarching title are two sub-titles, each bearing a letter of the alphabet, the first in uppercase and the latter in lowercase. The first poem in each pair has three stanzas; the second six, and each stanza consists of three lines. For example, the first canto, "1 I said to myself, Guillaume, it's time you came"—Guillaume Apollinaire (France), is the main title; the following pair of poems are titled: "A. If Apollinaire could come, so can I," and "a. The implications of 'I'." The 26 pairs of poems, from A to Z, correspond to the 26 letters of the English alphabet, creating a self-sufficient and independent space for unbounded creativity. A pair of poems is a small, self-sufficient poetic space; a poem cycle is a large, self-sufficient poetic space. This combination adheres to strict rules in formal construction, while allowing for unbounded freedom in the choice of content. Combining strict rules with ample freedom is, in fact, the fundamental principle that Lu Jian has long adhered to in his poetry, and it is also the fundamental principle that Chinese and even global poetry has handed down to us. This reminds us of Lu Jian's *Famous Cities and Gates*; it also reminds me of classical Chinese poetry, the Western sonnet, and, more importantly, the question of the ritual nature of poetry.

Undoubtedly, among all literary genres, poetry is a unique form. This genre is unique in that it is not merely a form of textual presentation but also a ritual entity, a field with a ritual medium. In this ritualistic field, the realities to which the text refers are either transformed, strengthened, or awakened in some way. When a poet and his subject enter this ritual field, he is no longer an ordinary person living in the secular world, but a poet immersed in poetic ritual and possessing poetic thought. Writing becomes a ritual act in this moment and place. Through this ritual act, the poet transcends the real world into another space, achieving personal reflection and meditation, and completing his poetic experience. It is important to note that this ritualistic aspect of poetry is more prominent in classical Chinese poetry, while modern poetry struggles to express this ritualistic aspect through formal expression. Since the space entered through ritual is a sacred space, it naturally contains many norms. These norms are repeatedly reflected in a poetic form, becoming an inherent, logical driving force behind the work and a totemic symbol for the poet's creative behavior and the formation of the work. Both classical Chinese poetry and Western sonnets fully utilize the formal dynamics and symbolic implications of ritual, while modern poetry has weakened this poetic dynamic and symbolism. For modern poetry, which tends more towards "thinking" and "criticism," the loss of this ritual formal dynamic should be a natural process. For the free dissemination of "thought" may not necessarily require the support of certain norms, or perhaps the free dissemination of "thought" itself is not suitable for excessive norms. However, if we consider this issue from the perspective of "poetry" rather than simply "thinking," and if we consider "thinking" within the context of "poetry," we may discover how crucial the ritual qualities of poetry are to its extraordinary and sacred nature. Placing thought within a ritualistic form, allowing it to retain its freedom and sensitivity, and allowing poetry to assume a ritualistic, totemic quality, is perhaps a valuable concept. Exploring this approach would be a valuable poetic act. Interestingly, Lu Jian not only does this, but does so with profound meaning. Perhaps Lu Jian didn't envision it in the way I suggest, but his exploration of ritual forms in his poetry has indeed provided us with much inspiration and enhanced the poetic quality of his work. He constructs a "field" for himself and his subjects, a field governed by strict order. Perhaps it is precisely because of this order that the poet's creative thought is afforded the greatest freedom.

Second, free utterance and unfettered contemplation.

Achieving freedom through rigorous order is, in fact, a common method used by Lu Jian. A systematic study of his poetry reveals that he seems to have long been aware of poetry's formalized nature. Compared to other literary genres, this formalized quality constitutes its most fundamental characteristic, and indeed its very essence. Through formalized presentation, the poet and his subject enter into a poetic, ritualistic celebration. In this poetic celebration—the writing process— the poet and his subject can no longer distinguish between subject and object, or between the poet and the poem. However, once the poet and his subject exit this ritualistic "field," they become ordinary mortals and ordinary worldly matters. Ordinarily, within this ritualistic "field," the poet's freedom of thought and the spatial and temporal connections of his speech should be limited. However, *Songs of a Resplendent Minor Poet* achieves tremendous freedom through its uniquely ordered and ritualistic formal construction. Furthermore, judging by the poet's creative attitude throughout the collection, not only does he achieve immense freedom, but he also presents a free-flowing discourse. If we examine the poet's poetic content, we will discover that he presents four-dimensional subjective space-time: the poet, the "minor poet," history, and reality. The poet freely shifts between the poet and the "minor poet," between history and reality, and between China and the world. Through this collection, the poet offers us a feast of unfettered thought. The poet's profound contemplation and sharp criticism are rare in contemporary Chinese poetry. The unique structure of this collection affords the poet immense freedom of thought. Consequently, each group of poems in the collection is like a meteor shower of ideas, naturally formed, brilliant, and resplendent. It's impossible to comment on every poem in the collection; we can only offer a few examples to capture the poet's poetic vision. Lu Jian's opening poem, "1 I said to myself, Guillaume, it's time you came— Guillaume Apollinaire," reveals the poet's understanding of the "I." Truthfully, the "I" has been a constant issue in Chinese poetry since ancient times. In classical Chinese poetic theory, there is no distinction between the realm of self and the realm of no-self. From the perspective of literati, the realm of no-self seems superior. This seems to be related to the fact that Chinese poetic aesthetics largely draw on Buddhist enlightenment and Taoist principles of "Tao follows nature" and "the great way is invisible." However, the "I" in classical Chinese poetry, whether implicit or explicit, is simply a matter of artistic realm. While some do distinguish between high and low in terms of "quality," this doesn't constitute a significant issue. If examined from a cognitive perspective, it can be considered a problem.

The concept of "I" became a major issue in poetry after modern poetry became a tool of revolution, particularly between the 1950s and 1980s. Poetry at this time either lacked the individual "I's" emotions and thoughts, or transformed it into a representative of the class. By the early 1980s, this issue was raised as an obstacle to modern poetry writing, leading to the concept of the "I writ large." Despite being "writ large," the "I" finally gained a legitimate place in poetry. From the "big I" to the "small I," and then to removing the upper body and writing with only the lower body, the "I" finally established a connection with one's own body.

In fact, since the 1950s, the issue of "I" has been a persistent obstacle for Chinese poets, a crucial concern for every poet aiming to make a difference in poetic creativity. In my view, all questions concerning "I" in modern Chinese poetry, from its beginning to end, are questions about "man." All understandings of "I" are, ultimately, questions about how to understand "man." Lu Jian begins this collection of poems with a search for self: "My vocation is to create the image of a contemporary poet/ Hundreds of times I must break it apart and shape myself// Countless are those who have come throughout the ages/...My mouth is filled with their words." Although Lu Jian said in poem A, "If Apollinaire can come, so can I," once he enters into poetic thought, he still faces the problem squarely: in front of those "tall and majestic" predecessors, he still had little room for the right to speak. Therefore, in the six stanzas titled "a," Lu Jian reaffirms his "I" by reiterating: "I am just myself, not the I of yesterday/ not the future I, not an idea of self,. not a definition, but a fleshly body." In this poem, the poet, seeking to present a truly authentic "I," goes from demonstrating his ambition with the phrase "If Apollinaire can come, so can I," to confronting the sages of past and present who have silenced "I" with their words, to recognizing the "I" as a physical body, to eating grains, learning culture, and understanding civilization, to directly declaring, "I am an enemy of tyranny, and at the same time/ a kindhearted adherent of Tolstoy's thought." The author's unrestrained writing, traversing ancient and modern times, China and the West, not only expresses the connection between "I" and the world, but also upholds his own national stance on the poet's spiritual and intellectual affiliation. He not only reveals the contradictions within himself, but also fully acknowledges his own willpower as a "contemporary poet" with a "strong reproductive energy," believing "If Apollinaire can come, so can I." Confronting reality and himself directly, Lu Jian's charm lies in his ability to confront the very nature of "I." In the poems under "2 I am a nobody, who are you? — Dickinson (USA)," Lu Jian deeply reflects on the proposition "Who would it be better to be?" Through the question of "who" should "I" become, the poet profoundly demonstrates the loss of "I" in modern society and the confusion and helplessness of the pursuit of self. The question "Who would it be better to be?" is itself a tragedy. No one is better, and the question of "better" does not exist. However, when the proposition "who am I" fails to embody the reality of "I," where lies the true self in the proposition "I am"? Lu Jian repeatedly reflects on this question from various perspectives throughout this collection. In the poems under 3 "After wearing out ten thousand books, my brush is moved as if by spirits" — Du Fu (China), the poet affirms the modern proposition of "I" "starting where the predecessors left off" through the double negation of the statement in C, "Neither a Brush Nor a Quill." Such a statement actually suggests we should be in an age of "Genesis," but what about the reality? "When our voices changed, suddenly we ran off in all directions/ No one could call out anyone else's name..." "Loss" is a common affliction of this era. "...like a poker game by a fireplace/ played by knights in a gothic castle along the Rhine/ You call for Rilke, he throws down a Derrida card// Wittgenstein gains the upper hand, being held by little "b"/ China's sun was blocked by a demon screen...we were careless/ and become fond of pre-paid cards from Carrefour and KFC." ("4 She is like an angel from heaven, descending to earth to show us miracles - Dante (Italy)") Lu Jian describes the reality of our age of self-loss. The loss of the poetic nature of Chinese culture is even more alarming. Yet, in many cases, we are self-satisfied, even complacent, in the process of self-loss and self-abandonment. Despite the poet's heroic declaration, "Even if the world has been patched together into a flat face, / the poet is destined to be the nose that stands out," the poet in today's world clearly recognizes that poetry "now yielding sovereignty to the God of commerce/ ...suffers the torment of a thousand cuts for us." Born into this world, perhaps earlier or later, in the distant past or in the distant future, if you are a poet, you will inevitably suffer the torment of purgatory; this is the poet's fate. If this world were free of contradiction and pain, free of ugliness and darkness, then this world would not need poets. Poetry and the secular world are a pair of contradictions, yet an inseparable whole. Poetry and the poet are constantly bound by the secular world, yet constantly striving to break free. It is in this process of struggle that the poet achieves self-realization. Either death or rebirth. "Who has died for me? For whom will I die?" Perhaps we don't know. "Perhaps I have spent my entire life completing a mistake," but "If my heart is upright, even remoteness is of no concern - Qu Yuan (Part 2).

From *Famous Cities and Gates, The Geneva Sun*, and *Warmth*, to *Songs of a Resplendent Minor Poet*, Lu Jian's poetry has progressed from pursuing human modernity to exploring the far reaches of the human spirit, then returning to the relationship between man and the land, ultimately presenting a comprehensive exploration of human issues. In essence, this journey has always revolved around a single goal: the question of man. If Lu Jian's early poems merely recorded human experiences in the real world—for example, if the tragedy in *Beauty, Innocence, Kindness, and Tragedy* were merely a beautiful "clash of forces" unrelated to ultimate human fate—then, in *Famous Cities and Gates* and *The Geneva Sun*, Lu Jian's poems explored the grandeur of the human spirit and humanity's fundamental misfortune within the vastness of the universe. In a sense, during this period, Lu Jian's understanding of man, society, and the universe remained separate: man was man, and the world was the world. However, in *Songs of a Resplendent Minor Poet*," for the poet in his resplendent minor role, man and the world are no longer separate; man is the world in its entirety. Here, we can use the titles of several cantos in Lu Jian's collection to draw connections, from which we can roughly see the poet's spiritual space-time and his far-ranging thoughts on the fate of mankind: 10 "Live where you live" – (Sweden) Hjalmar Guldberg; 11 "We are all responsible to all for all" -- (Russia) Dostoevsky; 12 " The reason I have great affliction is that I have a body" -- (China) Lao Tzu; 17 "We choose what we will make ourselves to be" -- (France) Sartre; 19 "The world is a stage, but the play is badly cast" – (British) Wilde; 20 "We can only enjoy the happiness we can understand" – (Belgian) Maeterlinck; and in the end, mankind can only sigh 26, "But I have…miles to go before I sleep/ And miles to go before I sleep" -- (USA) Frost. Under these grand themes, Lu Jian naturally presents us with the many trivial props and scenes of our current existence: flour and millet; Yu Jian's chubbiness; "The Old Man and the Sea"; women's skirts getting shorter and shorter; WeChat mini-blogs; "Tao Te Ching"; acting naive, acting cool, pretending to be somebody, or pretending to be a dead dog; having a son who is too young; losing too much weight in springtime; being a prisoner of one's own heaven-given disposition; a Liang Mountain bandit or Maoist raider; toxic milk powder, and so on. Both lofty philosophical reflections and the trivialities of life are part of us, part of ourselves and everything we create, from the mundanities of existence to the understanding of the profound destiny of our nation.

> *In the most telling verse line of the past 100 years*
> *a nation is boiled down to the pivotal line of a poem*
> *"...at its time of greatest danger"*
>
> *"...Its time of greatest danger" is not about 1911*
> *it is not 1937 or 1946; it is not 1989*
> *it is today, this very day in front of our faces* [1]
>
> *It is in the downfall of belief, the disarray of morals*
> *Even if a genius could create a brand new genre*
> *his precious fabric of words would only be taken for ravings*
> *(15, "The Chinese Nation Is at Its Time of Greatest Danger": (Tian Han)*

From a meticulous appreciation of life's details to a profound contemplation of the nation's fate, from humorous witty mockery to stern, pointed criticism—all of this constitutes the human element in Lu

Jian's poetry. Interestingly, even as he constantly ponders the question of humanity, the idea of humanity is itself hidden in his poetry, leaving only the song of a resplendent minor poet.

March 6, 2013, Zhengzhou

Shan Zhansheng is Editor-in-Chief of Henan Literature and Art Publishing House and a renowned literary critic.

A Long Masterwork of Contemporary Chinese Poetry

—A Brief Discussion on "Songs of a Resplendent Minor Poet"

by Xiong Guohua

Lu Jian's "Songs of a Resplendent Minor Poet" is 783 lines and 10,668 words long. It was praised by poet Hong Zhu online as "the most astonishing" and "my favorite Chinese long poem of 2012".[1] I believe that when examining the culture of an era, we should first examine the circumstances and competency of that era's poets, because true poets often represent the conscience of the era and the soul of the nation. Lu Jian's "Songs of a Resplendent Minor Poet" takes himself as a research case, analyzing the poet's situation in contemporary China, as well as his spiritual journey from confusion, anxiety, compromise, and reflection, to repentance, struggle, responsibility, and clarity. He uses irony to portray himself and his fellow poets, while also portraying our materialistic and bizarre era. He uses the knife of poetry to cut into the poet's heart disease and the cancer of the times. The profoundness of his intellectual content and his explorations and innovations in poetic form provide a new example for the successful creation in the long poem genre. It can be called a masterpiece of this genre in the contemporary Chinese poetry world.

1

From the perspective of a seasoned poet, Lu Jian surveys our "grove of literati" situated in poetry's contemporary ecology: the desire for and envy of literary awards; the imitation of translated works by Western masters; the tendency to slap things together in the era of microblogs; the awkward predicament of poetry dominated by commodification in the consumer age; the rapid rise to fame of the "sunflower coterie"; the "usefulness of expediency**" in poetry applied to branding of liquor, handbags, underpants, and sanitary napkins; the writing fads that shift from "running after those beautiful legs, with all he's got/from metaphors to refusing metaphors, then to/ the lower body school," then to the extreme pathology of "narration reduced to unbearable triviality/ then writing about culture until it's unrelated to culture/ writing poetry's history to the point of forgetting poetry"; and finally, "poetry's arm is dislocated at the shoulder/ she can not keep reality's top-heavy brain erect." The poet vividly exposes the various strange realities of the poetry world, not for the sake of momentary rhetoric, but to point out the problems within poetry and seek solutions, asking, like Heidegger, "What is the role of a poet in today's age?"

The poet, possessing a sense of responsibility, first uses himself as a target for self-mockery and others' ridicule, clearing out his personal life and inner waste, even refusing to shy away from family privacy. "Before my birth my father was already disabled/ My only legacy was a portion of original sin//My Petri dish: Mother, maternal uncle, husband of maternal aunt/ one minor intellectual, one right-leaning expert, suitable for inclusion/ in a public-private partnership, all their lives they didn't make noise//My main nutrient mixture: Great Leap Forward, Anti-Rightist Campaign/ Three-Year Famine, and ten tumultuous years of the Cultural Revolution/ In the name of doing great deeds, I was a locust scourging the countryside." Now, as a university professor, "when feeling happy I am a dolt, when suffering I am a poet//With teacher's pointer I stir the mix of nutrients and poison/which is knowledge, to force down throats of students, in exchange/for rice, fuel, oil and salt, plus a deep sense of unworthiness." He repents of "I thought of the harm I did to others, on purpose or not," "time after time betraying my own trust/ putting on an opera mask to go outdoors," and "the crimes we've committed against language." In an era of global turmoil and drunkenness, "Beijing also needs/ of someone to keep a vigil, to penetrate the world's vitals with his gaze." He resolved to "go back to being himself," "to keep my good-heartedness and inborn taciturnity," and to forge his own path. Since he couldn't like Heine declare that those who "say the name/ most worthy of renown, will say my name," and thereby fulfill his ambition to become a great poet, he might as well heed Borges' wise advice: "My ambition was to be a minor poet, and I have achieved it!" After experiencing repeated mental anxieties and soul-searching adventures, the poet suddenly realizes that only by seeing through and letting go can one find freedom, entering the clarity after the storm. "All of my hatred has been discarded, and envious pangs/ are like rice at the bottom of a crock during a famine/…A man on the road does not forget his dear brothers/ I give them blessings, and do not forget myself." Since even Borges was easily contented, let us strive to be "a group of resplendent minor little poets", stick to a poet's duties and conscience, and write poetic stanzas "for lowly humans and oneself/ softly offering canticles to ripe smells and heaven's favor"; let us "face heaven's vault, as our earthward aspect/ registers the precarity of this dusty world," which is what poets should really do.

2

Lu Jian uses poetry to paint a portrait of himself and of poets as a whole, clarifying numerous issues within poetry. In fact, the issues of poetry and those of our times are intertwined, like the relationship between a vine and a tree. While painting his own portrait, the poet also, consciously or unconsciously, paints a portrait of our times. After all, as a professor at China Communications University, and having somehow lived for over half a century and met countless people, Lu Jian presents us with an encompassing and complex landscape of our times in this long-form poem. Its content touches on history, culture, science, religion, philosophy, literature, ethics, politics, economics, education, sports, medicine, architecture, folklore, cooking, entertainment, marriage, and love, as well as   being rich in details and scenes of daily life. The poet traverses time and space, integrating Eastern and Western influences, touching on sources ranging from the ancient Egyptian *Book of the Dead* and the Greek epics of Homer to the Chinese sages Lao Tzu and Confucius; from primitive hunting to modern high technology; from ordinary people to heads of state like Obama, as well as the bizarre phenomena of our own time. Wherever the pen points, one can feel the force of "killing with one blow."

Take for instance, "the first right humans gained in the Garden of Eden/was the right to privacy", but now those who adhere to the counterculture first of all oppose the right to privacy, "People doing cultural studies often go in for mental masturbation/ In rural towns there's a buzz over sex toys; some websites/ host naked chatrooms; summer fashions reveal midribs and buttocks." Or consider the hype of cultural fashion, "academic show, reality show, a put-on show, a parody show/ a sharp-tongued show, a stuttering, tongue-tied show," or "act like a greenhorn, like you're cool, like you're stylish, like a dead dog," it leaves you between tears and laughter! Or consider the loss of sense of responsibility: "This morning at a hospital drop-in, the doctor said I was responsible/ for the cryptic cystitis in my belly, but he would only be responsible/ for receipt of payments. At dusk in the park my girl-friend stifled sobs/ because love can no longer be responsible for virginity." Such are the losses of social integrity and morality: "Lovers who once coupled in the wilds now call for hotel rooms/ We hear a harvester rumbling; wheat plants get their fill of chemicals/now that rapid growth is a route to the city for plump kernels// Gas stations and toll booths are closely spaced; physiques of singers/ are puffed up, and lip synching has a factory's worth of stage effects/ A neighbor girl who got a nose job appears outside your condo block." Concerned about the country and its people, the poet pleads for the people, loudly calling for "Disband the Crowd Control Office, cut down on taxes/ cut back on police, auxiliaries and doomsayers of pollution/ Let wages ride the up escalator and prices ride the down escalator." He sharply points out that the Chinese nation's "most dangerous moment... is when faith collapses and morality is in disarray." From the perspective of ecological holism, he profoundly argues that "Humanity grows like rampant weed// without conferring much value or meaning on this planet/ An honor for members of one group is poison for another."

Undoubtedly, the poet's profound and precise descriptions provide a comprehensive "electrocardiogram" of the ills of our time. This comprehensive overview of life is beyond the reach of the average "minor poet." The poem is exceptional in its depth and breadth of depiction of contemporary life, as well as its forceful critique of evils, possessing a soul-stirring power. While exposing the chronic ills of our times, the poet simultaneously ponders: What have I done in this era, and how can I save humanity? His search ultimately leads him to the remedy: "To encircle a whole city, it takes love/ To encircle all of planet earth, only love will do." It is "what Jesus spoke of as 'omnipresent,' moreso than/ cars, computers, guided missiles, more than spaceships/ more than the steel flowers from thousands of years of science/ and artificial bacteria put together by nano-technology." Love can dissolve hatred, redeem souls, and create beauty! "Let me hook love up to other people's hearts, to avoid ischemia

tachycardia, and clotting." He boldly voices a demand: "If the government cannot make love circulate like currency, it should give itself a day off!" He inherited Li Bai's contempt for the powerful: "Today's great men are like a grasshopper caught by a child's straw hat," and "Greatness is but the wind that blows through the world." If it doesn't benefit humanity and the planet, what is greatness? He reveres nature as much as he reveres the philosophy of love, extolling a hermit indifferent to fame and fortune. "I want to devote an entire chapter of literary history to Tao Qian, reciting 'Peach Blossom Spring' on Wangfujing Street, for all the people and plants under heaven to hear." He comese before us as a "resplendent minor poet" who is truly admirable and endearing.

3

As mentioned above, this epic poem spans vast chronological and spatial dimensions, encompassing nearly every aspect of social life. The question of which form to choose to convey such vast and weighty content is crucial for the author of the epic poem, a crucial factor determining the success of the work. Poetry, in terms of style, excels at lyricism but lags behind narrative. Previous epics mostly depicted a single character, a story, or eulogized a political party or nation. Their structure was often linear and concise. Their heavy narrative elements and straightforward language lacked poetic quality. This traditional epic structure and style are undoubtedly insufficient to capture the complexities of modern life and the subtleties of modern human experience. "Songs of a Resplendent Minor Poet" boldly innovates in poetic form, providing a successful model for epic creation.

This long poem has a unique structure. It is divided into 26 cantos according to the letters of the English alphabet, but the cantos are numbered using Arabic numerals 1 through 26. The verses are written entirely in Chinese characters. Each canto has two poems, the first listed by an upper case letter and the second by lower case. Each stanza consists of three lines, with three stanzas making up the first poem and six stanzas making up the second, meaning each canto consists of nine stanzas and 27 lines, creating a rigorous and orderly structure. I'm not entirely sure why Lu Jian wrote 26 chapters, just as I'm not entirely sure about the specific origins and meaning of the 26 letters in English. However, one thing is certain: all of English is spelled out using the 26 letters, forming a unique system of linguistic symbols. This allows us to glimpse Lu Jian's poetic intent: the 26 cantos of this long poem are self-contained (separately forming independent units and collectively forming a coherent whole), embodying a fusion of Chinese and Western elements in an encompassing way. This is one aspect.

Secondly, the poems under capital and lowercase letters are similar to the main melody and polyphony in music, with their attendant implications. In the European Middle Ages, religious music was mainly monophonic. During the Renaissance, as the divinity was de-emphasized and humanism revived, a place was gradually found for secular music. In the Baroque period, the great German musician Bach created a large number of polyphonic pieces. Two or more melodies "play simultaneously and form an organic whole that is interconnected. In terms of horizontal relationships. Each part has its own independence in terms of rhythm, emphasis, dynamics, starting and ending, and the rising or falling of the melody line. In terms of vertical relationships, each part forms a harmonic relationship with each other. Polyphonic music uses counterpoint as its main creative technique."[2] In Lu Jian's long poem, the poem listed by the capital letter is similar to the main melody, and the poem listed by the lowercase letter is similar to the polyphony. Generally speaking, the capital letters represent spiritual life, and lowercase letters represent secular life. In today's era, mass culture has an advantage, so the number of stanzas under lowercase letters is twice what is under capital letters. Spiritual, elite thoughts and secular, popular thoughts penetrate and cross-reference with each other, thus corresponding to the diverse and complex phenomena of social life.

Third, the title of each canto and the capital and lowercase titles under it form an intertextual relationship. All the titles are quotes from famous people in ancient and modern times, or famous poems and lines, which serve as a summary of the canto. "This issues a call to others, or it reminds one of a memory, thus establishing a channel of communication. An entire treasure house full of literary works are briefly reviewed and intertwined with my writing in the reader's mind."[3] This guides readers to follow the poet's thoughts into a new artistic space. The poems tagged by capital and lowercase letters in each chapter are generally based on the drift of the main title, from which they are extended and amplified. The poems tagged by capital letters are more spiritual, general and abstract, while the poems tagged by lowercase letters are more secular, specific and concrete. The three-level titles bear a stepwise correspondence to each other, causing the content to interweave, illuminate, metaphorize, interpret and expand. This forms a semantic field of multi-sensory, intertextual connections, similar to the harmony formed by the simultaneous sounding of multi-part melodies and harmonious counterpoints.

Fourthly, each stanza consists of three lines, a rare occurrence in long poems. The four-line stanza format, a long and familiar one, is a well-established format for both modern and classical poetry. In Tang Dynasty regulated verse, the quatrain is a standard four-line verse, while the eight-line, two-couplet regulated verse can be considered a variant of the four-line format. This structure of introduction, development, transition, and conclusion became a fixed mindset, and its rigorous rhythmic flow reflects the changing seasons and the stable life of a long-standing agricultural civilization. Modern life, marked by commodities and information, is ever-changing, and natural and man-made disasters are unpredictable. The psychological pressures, anxieties, trendiness, and desires of urban dwellers have long eroded the pastoral mood. In an era where psychological stability is unattainable, the poet strives to find inner fortitude through self-reinforcement, externalizing this fortitude in a precarious yet tenacious formal order. Transforming even-numbered stanzas into three-line stanzas may be a more effective approach, breaking with the four-line mindset while establishing a new formal order. Although three-line stanzas have been used by many people in modern poetry, it is rare to see a long poem of tens of thousands of words using three-line stanzas from beginning to end. It can be said that this is a creative use of the form. An example is as follows:

8. *In sadness I survey our present generation— (Lermontov)*

H. In Sadness Our Generation Surveys Lermontov

Academic show, reality show, a put-on show, a parody show

a.   sharp-tongued show, a show that fumbles for words

put on a ruminative look, a look of absurd hypothesizing

Put on a look of left and right body halves being unmatched

Act like a greenhorn, like you're cool, like you're stylish, like a dead dog

give it a poke and it will slink away over a wall

I was born from swaddling clothes, not out of mother's body

my intellect comes from truth and not from life

with sadness our present generation surveys Lermontov

b.   The Sunflower Manual for Winning Instant Fame

Step 1: Give myself a distinctive pen name

A poet in Shanghai could name himself "Waibai" [1]

and his poet-girlfriend could be called "Duqiao" [2]

Step 2: Starting at a top school, treat poetry as a movement

then stir up a big splash to make my name a hot commodity

that appears in big journals, weeklies and anthologies

Step 3: Don't offend leaders or plain folk. As the scene unravels

slog through the trash and invasive weeds; then when I become famous

wield a scalpel-like pen, noting little details to expose gross faults

Step 4: Study a foreign language. Even if I murder the pronunciation

my poems will conform to European syntax, for ease of translation

Best of all, have Mr. Li Li hand deliver them to contacts in Stockholm [3]

Step 5: Stand beside people who have hulking, strapping physiques

When people see them, they will notice me there

They will see embroidery; at the same time they'll see plain stitches

Step 6: Set myself in opposition to a certain now-deceased figure

Of course I'll appear as one whose intentions are wholly innocent

The heart bent on grand success has the focus of a fine needle

The title of the eighth canto quotes the famous line "I look with sorrow upon my generation" by the Russian writer Lermontov. The poem under the capital H draws upon this quote and uses it in a paradoxical way. Its nine lines satirize the hype and pretense of our time, characterized by affectation and deception, distortion of the truth, and the reversal of priorities. Thus, "In Sadness Our Generation Looks upon Lermontov" forms an intertextual relationship with the canto title. The first poem is more abstract, general, and "spiritual." The lowercase title, "The Sunflower Manual for Winning Instant Fame," references the martial arts codex "Sunflower Manual" from Jin Yong's novel *The Smiling, Proud Wanderer*, to satirize the various tactics used to achieve rapid fame in contemporary poetry. This relatively concrete, detailed, and "worldly" emphasis forms a counterpoint to the uppercase h title, further exposing, interpreting, and satirizing the unscrupulous pursuit of fame and fortune. It highlights the cultural and spiritual sorrow of our generation, while also forming an intertextual relationship that echoes the canto title. The juxtaposition of the three titles creates a multifaceted structure, in multidimensional spacetime, and a multifaceted dialogue within the poem. It breaks down the boundaries between history and reality, time and space, and East and West, examining and evaluating individual actions within a vast historical context. Its connotations are richer and deeper than a single title. The three-line stanza format breaks the stereotype of a four-line stanza, creating a concise, clear, and novel effect. Three lines can stand alone as a stanza, or they can be linked together according to how the reader punctuates them (as in the first and second stanzas above), allowing for greater flexibility and freedom of transition than a four-line stanza. Although not all cantos of the long poem are written according to the above pattern, appropriate variation, transposition and change can make the canto structure more colorful, so that it conforms to the aesthetic principle of order and variability.

Lu Jian wrote "Songs of a Resplendent Minor Poet" with the conscience of a poet, the pursuit of truth and a Rousseau-style spirit of confession. The profoundness of his thoughts, his concern and criticism of real life, his exploration of the relationship between man, nature and society, and his pursuit and questioning of the meaning of existence and the fate of mankind have brought us much beneficial inspiration and spiritual stimulation. In his thinking about poetry and people, and about people in their era, he was brave enough to explore and experiment, while working hard to find the fitting form of expression. Finally, he created a long poem structure with imposing scope, profound thoughts, rigor and wonder, and realized his long-standing poetic dream. "Even if the world has been collaged into a flat face/ the poet is destined to be the nose that stands out." We will remember Lu Jian's wonderful portrait of himself and the times.

References:

[1] Hong Zhu, "My Favorite Chinese Long Poems of 2012", http://blog.sina.com.cn/hongzhublog

[2] *Cihai·Art Volume*, Shanghai Dictionary Publishing House, 1980 edition, page 137. [3] Valéry Larbourg, "Blessed by Saint Jérôme," in *Intertextuality Studies*, by Tiffany Samoyaux (France), translated by Shao Wei, Tianjin People's Publishing House, 2003, p. 35.

Xiong Guohua is the director and professor of the Chinese Department of Guangdong Second Normal University, director of the Institute of Overseas Chinese Literature, and secretary-general of the International PEN Poets Club.

Mar.18, 2013

A Dantesque Questioning
and Redemption in the Wasteland of the Soul
—A Draft Essay on Lu Jian's Long Poem
"Songs of a Resplendent Minor Poet"

by Zi Wu

"Our world floats on a breath of air, past and present between the influence of two orbs." (Zhang Zhao, "Viewing the Sea") Poetry represents the commanding heights of an era's language and conscience, giving a textual sculpture of the heights of thought and aesthetics, and a true, concise, and vivid portrayal of a nation's spiritual history.

Lu Jian said, "My left hand holds poetry, my right hand grasps reality" (see Chapter 3 of the long poem). For over 20 years since the early 1990s, he has actively explored the diversity and possibilities of Chinese poetry's form, genre, and artistic form, achieving remarkable and substantial breakthroughs. As early as September 1992, after the publication of Lu Jian's poetry collection *Famous Cities and Gates* by the Cultural and Art Publishing House, I noted that Lu Jian had created a new genre: the poetry feature. His subsequent work, *34 Gifts* (May 2004), was also a successful work of the poetry feature genre. In artistic form and style, his poetry collections such as *Dr. Leleute in the SARS Period* (June 2003), *Bill on a Maple Leaf* (June 2006), *Tianlou, Tianlou* (October 2006), and *On the Sun of the Luo River* (April 2007) are all documentary poetry. It is no exaggeration to say that Lu Jian's poetry collections and documentary poetry series are both groundbreaking and constructive in the history of modern Chinese poetry.

Lu Jian's long poem "Songs of a Resplendent Minor Poet" (*Chinese Poetry*, March 2013), which he created not that long ago, is considered a classic long poem of contemporary China. In it, he draws on the epic structure and several artistic elements of Dante's *Divine Comedy*. With Eliot's acumen, depth, and grandeur, he draws on the perspective of modern poetry and the poet's introspective spirit to gradually approach and unfold an interrogation of the "wasteland of the soul" pervading society through self-examination. It should be pointed out that this brilliant and gorgeous long poem is not only a microcosm of China's contemporary poetry scene, but also the most direct reflection of the spiritual reality of people in modern society.

I. Structure: Borrowing the Form of the Divine Comedy, Integrating the Soul of Fugue (From Poetry as Healing to Cultural Redemption)

Structurally, Lu Jian's "Songs of a Resplendent Minor Poet" draws on the spirit of grand narrative in Dante's *Divine Comedy* while also incorporating the form of mathematics, being composed of letters and a rigorously specified matrix. The poem comprises 26 cantos, each divided into two sections (which can be considered analogous to the upper and lower halves of classical regulated verse), listed sequentially by 26 uppercase and lowercase English letters. Each canto has three three-line stanzas in the first section, and six three-line stanzas in the second section (for a total of 27 lines per canto), totaling 702 lines (excluding the canto and section titles). The poet ingeniously employs musical counterpoint to structure the poem, resulting in a poem resembling a rigorously structured and beautifully styled fugal suite or a sophisticated opera.

The poem dives straight into its central theme at outset. Just as Dante's first encounter in "Inferno" was with the great Roman poet Virgil (who guided Dante through Hell and Purgatory), Lu Jian's first encounter in the poem's first chapter is the French poet, novelist, critic, and playwright Apollinaire (who profoundly influenced avant-garde movements in literature and art, including Cubism, Futurism, Dadaism, and Surrealism). Lu Jian's placement of Apollinaire at the head of the more than 20 Chinese and international cultural figures in the poem is profoundly significant. He hopes to draw wisdom and strength from Apollinaire for the innovation. In the poem's opening verse, Lu Jian writes, using the traditional mode of rhapsodical poetry from the *Book of Songs*, "My vocation is to create the image of a contemporary poet / I must break and reshape myself a thousand times."

Since the New Poetry Movement ended in the late 1980s, Lu Jian reflected deeply and dedicated himself to exploring a path forward for Chinese modern poetry. With the unique acumen of a scholar-poet, he discerned the intellectual impetuosity and weakness that had plagued the Chinese poetry scene (and indeed the literary world as a whole), a lack of profound cultural experience, a tendency toward frivolous literature and consumerist language, and the resulting downward spiral of poetry (e.g., low-brow poetry, writing about the lower half of the body), as well as the proliferation of online jargon. Like a poetic "prophet," Lu Jian grasped this with exceptional depth. "Ah Poetry// once the God of morality set his sights on her/ now yielding sovereignty to the God of commerce/ she suffers the torment of a thousand cuts for us." (Canto 6).

Lu Jian's life and poetic journey truly reflect the overall spirit of the Chinese poetic community. In his poem, he self-deprecatingly writes: "...though I know I am still a minor figure// I got the food and clothes a child needed to grow, and my lower body/ swelled along with my intellect, then I devoured masses of books/ until fingers dancing on keys took the place of handwriting." "Often it borders on plagiarism, with occasional flashes of inspiration." He wisely positions himself this way: "Picking up where past masters left off/ as has been the case since Baudelaire's time."(Canto 3); despite the fact that "All other writing we've done, no matter how diligent/ aside from building up proficiency, was all futile effort" (Canto 13).

He unhesitatingly plunges into the contemporary poetry scene with scalpel-like, cogitative language, diagnosing the current state of poetry: "...As the scene unravels/ slog through the trash and invasive weeds..."

(Canto 8). In fact, outstanding poets like Lu Jian have unshirkingly shouldered the important task of enlightenment (both poetic enlightenment and human and cultural enlightenment) of the May Fourth Movement. At a time when "desolation is in my eyes," his inner feelings resemble those of "a warrior who has yet to make his debut" (Chapter 10).

What strikes us most is Lu Jian's description of the universal "desertification" of the modern human soul. In terms of information dissemination, the development of online media has, on the one hand, been a cultural catalyst, facilitating the formation of an "information superhighway." On the other hand, it has unexpectedly become a breeding ground for information duplication, emotional duplication, and even cultural duplication. This has led to two consequences: first, a decrease in original cultural products, and second, a dissolution of culture and information itself. Thus, information duplication → information overload → intellectual exhaustion has become a vicious cycle of "information dissolution" (and intellectual dissolution).

1. Replication of Information: Technology = Preservation?

Through Lu Jian's poetic lines, we can sense the cold light glinting from the knife edge of his language. "Our generation looks at Lermontov with sorrow." This cold gleam—the "desolation" in the eyes and the context of modern people—points directly to the "wasteland" of the soul. "As I reach out, is it to take something for myself,/ or to hand over what is needed by another person?" (Canto 10) Could it be that "scientific intellect invents refrigeration technology/ to preserve the 'freshness' of stale old stories" (Chapter 5)?

In the second chapter of the poem, Lu Jian, channeling the legendary American poet Emily Elizabeth Dickinson, asks: "I am a nobody, who are you?" In an age of repetitive information replication, the poet spends every day "In a flash of thought, in calendar pages eaten by silverfish larvae/ in ledgers, in manuals, while making my way through a crowd." All we can do, however, is to preserve ourselves amidst this "vaulting skies and hazy wild views" by detaching ourselves from the world—by "...a carefree life/ open to the light..." (Chapter 10). This has undoubtedly become our only "choice."

Lu Jian then seamlessly shifts from metaphysical philosophical propositions to the concrete details of existence: "but my son is still growing and springtime is scrawny"; "I look at my pay slip: one is one, two is two / Around me, there is a lack of vast, rugged nature" (ibid.). This is the common fate of this generation (including poets). Perhaps it can be called "replication" (or preservation) of fate. Not only must we shoulder the hardships of supporting our families through the roles of husband, father (and son), but we must also shoulder the contemporary mission of cultural and human enlightenment and the construction of new poetry. To accomplish these two tasks, we must "scientifically preserve" the constantly evolving online context and poetic language. The replacement rate of young poets and the elimination of online language is so rapid, even faster than that of pop singers.

a. Language replication: nouns and tooth decay

In the internet age, people have become accustomed to living in a programmed, mediated environment. When language and information are repeatedly replicated and copied, vocabulary naturally becomes a mask. Facing this phenomenon, Lu Jian calmly writes with his characteristic humor:

Among Tang poets there was a Li Bai ("Li the White")

who could just as well have been Li the Black, and in our time

Gao Xingjian [1] *could have been French, and what would it matter?*

(Canto 2)

At some point in time, people became so obsessed with "feeding language so much candy its nouns suffered tooth decay// even giving their subjects breast enlargements and tissue grafts/ doing reconstructive surgery, slicing and dicing concepts, like food courts/ that serve "deep fried ice cream..."" (ibid.). The falsity of life leads to the distortion and masking of language, and the falsity of language leads directly to poetry's distortion or betrayal of life.

b. Emotional replication: "way" and "principle" → homosexuality?

In reality, many things appear unrelated on the surface, but in reality, all things coexisting in this world are inherently interconnected. As early as 1963, American meteorologist Edward Lorenz discovered this phenomenon known as the "butterfly effect" in chaos theory. He famously proposed: "A butterfly in the Amazon rainforest of South America, by randomly flapping its wings, can cause a tornado in Texas two weeks later." This theory of the butterfly effect is said to have been inspired by Zhuangzi's dream of the butterfly, which occurred over 2,200 years ago.

Similarly, Lu Jian was inspired by the line from Zhuangzi's "On the Equality of Things": "I wonder if Zhou dreamed he was a butterfly? Or if the butterfly dreamed he was Zhou?" In daily life, frequently used words like "country" and "people" often become the most misappropriated. This is a spontaneous collective emotional replication of collective concepts. "For instance ideas of "nation" and "state"// once two distinct terms, are mingling currents like Jing and Wei rivers/ Now even words like "way" and "principle" have a homoerotic fling [2]/ from "the knight on yonder bank" to a murky mingling of waters." (Canto 9).

Lu Jian's poetry is characterized by connecting serious stems and leaves with humorous buds. He even duplicates and pastes data on human emotions into the issue of homosexuality (according to authoritative statistics from the World Health Organization, 4 to 6 out of 100 people are homosexual)."Coal briquets are black' and 'Lantern Festival Snowballs are white/ both are true, but each speaks for itself without mentioning/ that both of them are round" (Canto 17). Such is the way Lu Jian's humor silently permeates every line and semantic construct.

2. Junk information: excess / obscuration of discourse

Undoubtedly, the verification of philosophical questions ultimately comes down to mathematical methodology. Similarly, when describing the experience of being in a context of information overload, Lu Jian states it quantitatively: "I've eaten a thousand bowls of rice, to put a frame of aluminum/ on a Rembrandt painting; I have taken one hundred showers/ to dip the wolf-hair brush of Huang Binhong in ink" (Canto 7). And the most ironic thing is that human civilization experiences both pain and joy in this way—

> *Just when Bada Shanren's birdsong was being heard*
> *T.S. Eliot fainted away in his twilight*
>
> *Usain Bolt cut 0.16 seconds from Asafa Powell's record*
> *but philosophers turn back to study Lao Tzu's sublimity*
> *Across my desk are spread 17 editions of Tao-teh Ching*
> *(Ibid.)*

Information overload has led to a massive outpouring of junk information (including junk poetry and junk culture). "Language has become a breath / Rhyme has become garbage, tumbling and pervasive" (Chapter 15 of the epic poem); "One, two, three, four, five, six, seven / Numbers, after giving voice, become material desires," and "narratives have been reduced to triviality, to the point of being irrelevant to culture / The history of poetry has been written to the point of forgetting poetry" (Canto 16).

Irrelevancy to culture and forgetfulness of poetry not only obscures them but at the same time is a self-obstruction by cultural communicators and poets. This is perhaps something they never anticipated when disseminating culture and writing poetry. Thousands of pieces of information are drowned out and "formatted" mid-route when they are sent out. As a field of discourse is generated, it is immediately obscured by a larger, invisible field and order (including the mutual obstruction between various systems of discourse).

3. Intellectual Exhaustion: The Formation of a Spiritual "Wasteland"

The loss, desolation, and spiritual exhaustion of an entire generation inevitably led to the formation of a modern spiritual "wasteland." Thus T. S. Eliot, looking "into the heart of light, that silence," saw the entire society as "desolate and empty as the sea" ("The Burial of the Dead," Chapter 1, *The Waste Land*). He contrasts the wasteland with Baudelaire's Paris and Dante's inferno. He incorporates mythological, anthropological, Christian, and Eastern religious imagery, focusing on the scene of London under the black fog of a winter morning: an illusory city. This scene reflects and symbolizes the spiritual crisis of the entire Western world after World War I. Eliot's description of London 90 years ago in *The Waste Land* (written between 1919 and 1922 and first published in the literary journal *The Criterion* in October 1922) has unfortunately become a prophetic reflection of the contemporary "wasteland" of the modern soul.

This is the harsh linguistic and cultural reality that unfolds daily in the information age. Lu Jian, similarly, employs Eliot's "wasteland" consciousness and poetic wisdom to illuminate contemporary Chinese poetry, and even modern society as a whole, within the same context. Glimpsing into the "desert" of modern man's soul, he observes: "Yet flowers cannot protect their scent, the beauty of poppies/ decrees they must grow somewhere secluded; the trailing curls/ of a long-bearded violinist will someday snap his neck" (Canto 9). Lu Jian cannot help but sigh a heavy and helpless sigh, because: "...Jorge Luis Borges/ for the sake of light, had to lose his penetrating eyesight." "Soldiers died for generals, the living died so coffins might be made" (Canto 6).

Based on this, Lu Jian has well-founded evidence to point out the pathology of contemporary poetry: "A poet is responsible for the psoriasis of words and phrases/ for when the spleen of language are not well, its diet unvaried/ leading to osteoporosis and chronic debility." (Canto 11) Modern people's spiritual constitution is thus gradually degenerating, from words and phrases to the spleen and stomach, and finally to bone tissue.

From the inner spiritual level of poetry, the "spiritual wasteland" of modern people expressed in Lu Jian's poems resembles the scenes of physical and spiritual suffering and their overall symbolism described in Dante's "Inferno" (the nine circles of Hell). In terms of the poem's structure, from "Chapter 1: 'I said to myself, Guillaume, it's time you came'" (Guillaume Apollinaire) to "Chapter 8: 'I look sorrowfully at our generation'" (Lermontov) it is equivalent to the "Inferno" of the Divine Comedy. From "Chapter 9: 'If only my heart is upright, even remoteness is of no concern'" (Qu Yuan) to "Chapter 17: 'We choose what we will make ourselves to be'" (Sartre) is equivalent to the "Purgatory" of The Divine Comedy; then, from "Chapter 18: 'Cut bamboo, assemble bamboo, make clay pellets, chase living flesh'" (*Ancient Ballads*, Spring Autumn Period) to "Chapter 26: '...And miles to go before I sleep/ and miles to go before I sleep'" (Frost) is equivalent to the "Paradise" of *The Divine Comedy* (in terms of chapter structure only).

Admittedly, the third section of the long poem does not depict paradisical life corresponding to *The Divine Comedy*. (Lu Jian merely raises the question through poetry; as a poet, his poetry itself does not incur or undertake direct responsibility for the redemption of humanity and culture for the entire society). Even so, whether human civilization has ever developed a "paradise" of humanity and culture up to now and culture remains an unending riddle of the Sphinx. However, Lu Jian is grateful to have chosen Junna, a girl from Rizhao, Shandong, as his Beatrice. "She seemed like an angel from heaven, descending to earth to show us miracles." (Dante) It was precisely this Junna who "...with her devoted heart wished to prove/ that everyone is worth cherishing." At the same time, she made the poet Lu Jian feel that " the world would be different from before," so he "would no longer be doubtful of poetry, of beauty." "My wife bumped me and asked 'Were you in love with her?'/ I thought a bit, and answered 'yes'..." (Canto 18)

As Lu Jian's pen moves, his gaze sweeps across the ancient and modern worlds, from poetry to society, from China to the world, capturing the increasingly objectified, refined, and numbed souls of an entire generation in the context of high technology and commercialization. As "the boom of time swings, perhaps history precedes/ and the future is behind, or perhaps the other way around/ Perhaps I've spent a lifetime making one mistake." (Canto 7) As a poet with an intellectual historical mission, Lu Jian sees ever more clearly that:

Ideology ascends in a spiral... nationalities, states, isms

schools and techniques of poetry vs. its essence and principles

whorls that formed my palmprint, borrowing the name of freedom

(Ibid)

Thus, Lu Jian offers a suggestive "remedy" for the salvation of Chinese poetry (and indeed the entire literary world)—a redemption not only for poetry, but also for culture, and even more so for the souls of modern people: "Written words, like human beings, can be cured by bloodletting/ Poetry's axe chops down, words bleed at that moment/ Their bleeding coincides with my falling, bruited by swirling dust." (ibid.). It is through this "bleeding"---which is cultural, linguistic and ideological—that the goal of self-salvation can be truly achieved.

II. The Order of Word Images: Genes of Tradition and Cultural Destiny (From Self-Interrogation to Interrogation of a Generation)

In this long poem Lu of Jian writes of a generation in microcosm and extends that to the joys and sorrows, ups and downs, and desolation of human life in general. "Teasing the thread of events, we see our lives/ nebulous, or pale and panicked lives// Certain veins of content are laid out by fate, and thus/ one may be touched by one's own or by another's writing/ Fate's size is none other than our own size." (Canto 13).

1. The Inescapable Family Code: Agrarian Civilization + Confucianism

Lu Jian's poetry is sometimes startlingly calm! On the one hand, he bravely acknowledges his own inheritance of tradition (ethnic and cultural elements, etc.), and the congenital deficiencies, even the malnutrition, of this generation. On the other hand, he is forced to self-deprecately say: I am "...not an idea of self/ not a definition, but a fleshly body" Even though some may "say my skull is made of iron/ my torso and hands are wood, my legs/ are shaped from terra cotta..." (Canto 1).

Each of us carries this common family code, with its genealogical elements, inertia, and helplessness. "Now I'm huge and now tiny; in youth not having seen much/ at forty still bewildered; at fifty not knowing heaven's command/ living on and on until I've lived myself...into the shape I'm in." (Canto 2)

In contemporary Chinese poetry, no poet or critic has ever been as gracious as Lu Jian, a doctor with excellent medical ethics (and, by the way, a descendant of a Qing imperial physician), who so clearly and accurately articulates the social composition, cultural texture, linguistic abilities, and millennia-old agricultural traditions of this generation with such compassion, composure, and responsibility. And he does so in the form and language of poetry—

My staple foods are flour, rice and corn
along with Confucian and Taoist writings
Through translation I savor Western cultural bread

I am a product of agrarian ways, swept up
by machines and pushed headlong towards computers
taking care to protect my delicate lower ribs

I maximize my strengths in front of others
I am an enemy of tyranny, and at the same time

a kindhearted adherent of Tolstoy's thought

(Canto 1)

The Chinese nation's millennia-long cultural DNA has been deeply ingrained in every successor, including poets. As Lu Jian summarizes it: Our family code is "staple foods: flour, rice, and corn," and "Confucian and Taoist writing." It's "in translation" that we can "savor bread and Western culture." We are "products of an agricultural civilization," "...swept up by machines and pushed headlong towards computers/ taking care to protect our delicate lower ribs." Lu Jian's description is incredibly vivid and breathless!

2. The Distance Between Poetry and Life and the Poet: The Linguistic Relationship

The distance between poetry and life has always been the primary criterion for determining the importance and value of a poem or a poet. So, "How far can a poem take us? Or should I say/ ...what is our distance from a poem?" Lu Jian clearly sees this: "I often think the authors of *Book of Songs* and 'Ode to an Orange'/ were making fun of current writers; in fact when writing those odes/ they had no time to find fault; they

Needless to say, Lu Jian possessed a discerning perspective on the history and aesthetics of poetry. To use a Pekingese expression, Lu Jian's mind was as clear as a mirror. He not only had a thorough understanding of the relationship between poetry and life, but also a precise and precise grasp of the relationship between poetry and the poet. He gained valuable insights from his examination and analysis of classical poetry. "As for Tang poets— their talent lay in aesthetic charm, like a bevy of maids/ busily attending to their mistress' toilette, applying foundation and rouge/ using adjectives as ornament to heighten the elegance of words// to such a painstaking degree they nearly got on their mistress' nerves/ Later literati took the lessons to heart, and learned them with a vengeance."(Ibid) Lu Jian's humor often makes one laugh.

Even Tang poetry, revered as the classic form of Chinese poetry, harbors the taint of "fabrication" and "separation." In the online era's "copycat" poetry workshop, the distance between poem and poet becomes even more ambiguous and unpredictable, sometimes seeming worlds away, other times approaching "zero" (referred to as "zero friction" and "zero distance," hence the emergence of zero-degree narratives and Yu Jian's "Zero File," among others). As a result, even Lu Jian, with his clear mind, sometimes seems a bit helpless: "I know what I'm doing," yet at the same time, "I (don't) know/what I'm doing." (Canto 2) Ultimately, the relationship between poem and poet boils down to a linguistic one (Lu Jian calls this poetic generative relationship "language in costume," and uses it as the title for the second part of Canto 9).

a. Physical Distance: Original Sin + Culture Medium.

In Lu Jian's long poem, physical distance embodies its increments verbally through the fleshly body. "The reason I have great worries is because I have a body; if I have no body, what worries do I have?" This means that we worry because we have a self; if we forget the self, what worries do we have? The so-called "no body" here actually refers to the state of "no self." Once a person reaches this state of no self, there are no worries.

In fact, physical distance is a kind of real distance. It is both a temporal and a spatial form. The poet Hong Zhu once said, "Rather than saying the world is made up of matter, it's better to say it's made up of a variety of words. Words have become stand-ins for things."

My past incarnation was a sickly spermatozoa
Before my birth my father was already disabled
My only legacy was a portion of original sin

My Petri dish: Mother, maternal uncle, husband of maternal aunt
One minor intellectual, one right-leaning expert, one suitable member
of a public-private partnership, all their lives they didn't make noise
(Canto 12)

Here, the weak spermatozoa refers to this generation's congenital deficiencies; "original sin" actually refers collective fate: "My main nutrient mixture: Great Leap Forward, Anti-Rightist Campaign/ Three-Year Famine, and ten troubled years of the Cultural Revolution/ In the name of great deeds, I was a locust scourging the countryside." (Canto 12)

Lu Jian's introspective sincerity almost approaches the "confessional" sincerity of the great French Enlightenment thinker, philosopher, and writer Rousseau. In his poetry, he relentlessly reveals and analyzes his own and his contemporaries' "family histories" from the perspectives of history and the humanities.

b. Psychological Distance: Fool + Poet

Lu Jian's value lies in his profound understanding of not only his nation's time-honored and enduring cultural and poetic traditions, but also his thorough study of the composition of this culture and the specific cultural genes, contemporary elements, and linguistic heritage of Chinese poetry. This is the prerequisite for achieving great poetry and classics.

Lu Jian frankly admits: These "language animals" (people who write poetry in their native language), who coexist and interact with the material world, "are fools when they are happy, poets when they are sad" (Canto 13). As the saying goes, "History creates heroes, and heroes also create history." And all history is inevitably influenced by the shadow and driving force of war and hunger. Consider the generation described by Lu Jian:

> *Pupils dilated in eyes glaring green from hunger*
> *I was in fear of everyone, I had contempt for everyone*
> *even in nocturnal emissions I kept abusing lovely females*
>
> *With no chance to study, I'd have entered my own prison*
> *or gone off to a bandit hideout, into a maw engorged*

with the once-decent inhabitants it had ingested

(Canto 12)

Lu Jian even uses the lyrical subject (the potential protagonist) of the poem to say, "My delicate, uncallused hand could sting like a poison arrow" (ibid.). In fact, history, both in China and abroad, is often driven by a group of people who alternate between foolish and insane. According to the World Health Organization, over 60% of the world's 7 billion people suffer from varying degrees of mental illness. A significant number of these individuals recover later in life. This means that mentally ill individuals and lunatics can be found in all walks of life and professions. Politicians, a high-risk group of machinators, are particularly vulnerable. According to the New York Times, three psychiatrists, Dr. Jonathan Davidson, Dr. Katherine Connor, and Marvin Swartz of Duke University Medical Center, conducted extensive research and found that between 1789 and 1974, nearly half of all US presidents (a staggering 37) suffered from varying degrees of mental illness at some point in their lives.

c. The Distance Between Word and Image: The Beauty of Incompleteness

The distance between word and image, between language and poetry, is actually a psychological distance. "The laurel that crowned Homer was handed down in relay/ to crown another Homer. He himself would never see/ that laurel crown, what he saw was his own inner darkness." (Canto 2) Like Du Fu, his focus "always lies within the boundaries of classicism."

Lu Jian says, "things that reach extremes have beauty hiding/ in them, the edge of a sword's blade, the foot of Cinderella// the round edge of Venus' severed arm..." (Canto 9) This is what is called "incomplete beauty." Like Baii Yang enumerating the ugly heirlooms of his household, he writes—

Among poets of our time, those with long necks were called

Young A, Young B, Young C, Young D; those with shorter necks were called Cat, Dog, Little Fish or Little Shrimp. At first

we went naked, making a ruckus all day long, then later

when our voices changed, we abruptly ran off in all directions

No one was able to call anyone else by name

(Canto 3).

This is Lu Jian-esque humor: first, it draws from life (including specific details, drawn from here and there), all of them effortlessly captured; second, it is highly abstract and concise; and third, its language is masterfully refined, both witty and thought-provoking.

3. Interrogation, Beginning with a "Cry for Help" (The Cry of the Bones)

In terms of the language and production of his poetry, Lu Jian faced psychological pressure and linguistic anxiety similar to other members of his generation as they confronted the "shadow of death." "Dante stands at the apex of an "A", gazing down on humans/ on their paths of living and dying; I stand in the trough of a "V"/ sunk in an abyss, calling out right and left for rescue." (Canto 4). Clearly, this is a cry from the depths of a deep crisis.

The failure and death of language play out daily as a routine. Barely a poem is completed, it dies in the ocean of information, in the desert of the soul. Only a poet who refuses to sink into oblivion and bravely takes responsibility would issue this cry for help—for language, for self, and for poetry!

a. Dismantling One's Own Bones and the Bones of Fellow Poets

"Some say I'm too serious, putting on airs of a foreign literary figure/ I paste quotes from Western thinkers on the walls of my flat/ and peer at the world from behind the shoulders of a master." "...Some say my face/ is an expressionless portrait, which I parade about holding it up// with my neck. My sinitic language is mixed with phonetic spellings/

Due to an innate sense of lack, I cannot help being like this." (Canto 4) From the scapula (also called the pipa bone) of the master's shoulder to the cervical vertebrae in his own neck, from "peering" to "expressionless face," Lu Jian dismantles his own bones, and thereby sees through the bones and confidence of his fellow poets.

b. The Quality of Bones or Their External Display: Showmanship

The development of online media and the rise of popular culture have brought with it the rise of showmanship as a fashion. Just as "Academic shows, reality shows, showmanship, parody shows/ shows of eloquence and tongue-tied shows/ put on a ruminative look, a look of absurd imaginings//Act like the left and right body halves are unmatched /Act like a greenhorn, like you're cool or stylish, act like a dead dog." (Canto 8).

From education and culture to society as a whole, the pursuit of profit has led to a decline in morality and the deterioration of human nature. "...listen to educational institutions losing hope/ Cover your ears and crawl into a haystack, you'll still hear cries for help." (Canto 16) Faced with this reality and phenomenon, only introspection can awaken humanity's conscience and moral integrity. It is this patriotic introspection of Lu Jian that illuminates his character, his language, and his sincere poetry. "With teacher's cane in hand I stirred the mix of nutrients and poison/ which is knowledge, to pour down throats of students, in exchange/ for rice, fuel, oil and salt, plus a deep sense of unworthiness// So very common, yet it was heart-wrenching/ I think of the harm I did to others, on purpose or not/ If they were not fellow patients they were loved ones." (Canto 13)

c. The Bones of Time: Calcium Deficiency → Osteoporosis → Fate

Time and history are relentless. As latecomers and inheritors of human civilization, we are fortunate, yet we also bear the double misfortune of a fate predetermined by cultural destiny, shaped by our genes, and rewritten by our environment. As Lu Jian himself summarizes the linguistic chain generated by "time units": from "unvaried diet" to "calcium deficiency," then from "osteoporosis" to "physical debility" (Canto 11); as a result, "...a host of genes have been altered// and budding life sapped of zest."(Canto 15)

Lu Jian never conceals the embarrassment and helplessness of this generation of poets. "Countless were those (cultural pioneers) who came down through the ages," and many of them have become deeply ingrained in our blood and "have never disappeared." "There was a time they wept, laughed, rejoiced, despaired/

they came to worry for us or ridicule us. They are loved ones yet have// nothing to do with us, they loom beyond us, stern and aloof/ sometimes even leaking away between our fingers/ The language they used fills our mouths." (Canto 1).

The problem lies precisely in the fact that these cultural pioneers are both "our relations" and have "nothing to do with us." They are our "relations" because their genes flow through our blood; they have "nothing to do with us" because we cannot replicate or repeat them in an unchanging manner in cultural evolution. However, the overly recessive nature of these genes creates endless challenges and crises for their successors in cultural innovation.

Indeed, "Suppose a nation's top intellects were struck by successive pathologies/ brains cobwebbed, degraded and debased, telling lies without restraint" (Canto 15); and "...the arm of poetry is dislocated at the shoulder/

she can not keep reality's top-heavy brain erect," and "only self-esteem is like a clearing cloth that is still not too grimy/ should we use it to make a flag or a pair of underpants?" (Canto 21, "Record the Crimes We Have Committed against Language") Lu Jian's poetic fate mirrors the fate of the entire community of contemporary Chinese poets. We almost hear the clashing of their bones against the bones of time, the clash of swords as they grapple and battle with their own cultural genes and the current contextual order.

III. Style: Creating a Classic Long Poem

(Lu Jian's Unique "Pan-Narrative" Contribution)

"What is the role of the poet in an age of scarcity?" Heidegger's resonant words constantly echo in Lu Jian's ears. In this anti-poetic age, poetry and the very existence of poets face unprecedented and severe challenges! Some claim that far more people write poetry than read it, even declaring that "poetry is dead." "People who study culture frequently indulge in sexual fantasies" (Canto 5). However, intellectuals with conscience (including poets) are destined to always be bound by responsibility, conscience, and kindness. Accordingly, Lu Jian writes without hesitation in Canto 6: "Even if the world has been patched together into a flat face / It is the poet's fate to be the nose that stands out." Similarly the American poet Swenson faced the colloquial trend that dominated the American poetry scene in the mid-twentieth century (primarily from the Beat Generation and the confessional school), yet remained resolute and confident. She believed that only "poetry can help people maintain their true essence."[8]

From the perspective of artistic ontology, Lu Jian's "Songs of a Resplendent Minor Poet" is a long poem that looks upward and confesses downward. It is a poem about a poet who experienced a profound psychological crisis and then rose up, issuing a warning call to society. It is a poem about the poet's struggle and diligent exploration after the cultural collision and linguistic friction with the realities of life. It is the most pure and resolute poem of spiritual redemption in Chinese poetry since Haizi. In this unique poem, it is easy to see Lu Jian's increasingly mature and unique artistic style.

1. Classic "Grand Narrative" Structure

The success of this epic poem stems primarily from its exquisite, elegant, and architecturally beautiful structure. It can be said that Lu Jian, painstakingly crafting this epic poem, had previously spent at least twenty years exploring and preparing for "pan-narrative" poetry. His transition from a series of feature poems to a series of documentary poems was, in essence, an artistic warm-up or prelude to writing this long poem with a "grand narrative" quality.

On the one hand, Lu Jian condenses the monumental structure of the "Divine Comedy" trilogy (a total of 14,233 lines) into 26 chapters listed by letter (a total of 702 lines). On the other hand, he also makes Eliot's "wasteland" consciousness permeate the poem's content and ideological themes. Lu Jian defines his own psychological and poetic orientation as "like Frost, a poet of perception, emotion and gratitude," "who measured country roads beneath his feet/ got his finger on the pulse of living, to utter it.// He returned to the root of things…" "…Pacing along field borders/ craning his neck at starry reaches so supremely vast// For lowly humans and himself he wrote poetic stanzas/ softly offering canticles to ripe smells and heaven's favor/ in daily observances, as he passed through the ribcage of time." (Canto 26).

Each chapter of the poem consists of two parts: a "theme poem" (the upper verse) and a "counter-theme poem" (lower verse). The capitalized "theme poem" consists of nine lines and three stanzas, while the lowercase "counter-theme poem," a polyphonic form, consists of eighteen lines and six stanzas. The theme introduced in the "counter-theme poem" can also be seen as an artistic extension, variation, presentation, development, and re-enactment of the "theme poem." This unique line structure, consisting of one odd-numbered verse (nine lines) and one even-numbered verse (eighteen lines), is undoubtedly a reference to and adaptation of the "one yin, one yang" principle of Chinese Taoist philosophy.

In the grand narrative of his *Divine Comedy*, Dante not only explores every aspect of ancient social life, encompassing politics, economics (including finance), religion, law, education, culture, art, history, geography, and natural disasters, but also includes numerous personages from past eras. Similarly, Lu Jian's "Songs of a Resplendent Minor Poet," in addition to over 20 Chinese and international celebrities who serve as chapter titles, also features "I" and numerous figures from ancient and modern China and abroad. His work touches on politics, economics, education, culture, art, law, medicine, love, ethics, morality, the quality of the nation, and even the internet, supermarkets, the "Panfeng Sword Contest," Sanlu milk powder, forced demolitions, nude chats, environmental protection, and price issues. Lu Jian touches on nearly every social issue of concern. This epic poem, comprising just over 700 lines, is practically a chronicle of contemporary Chinese customs and cultural practices. The greatest success of this long poem lies in its ingenious use of this unique structure to encompass these extensive and unrelated fields, categories, and scenes and details of life within a single work. Through it, we can see the profound intellectual trains of thought, the artistic amplitude and rigor of this scholar-poet, along with his well-thought-out intentions.

2. Polyphonic Techniques and the Charm of Fugue

Polyphonic music originally referred to multimodal music composed of several parts, as opposed to monophonic music; later. It referred to music composed of multiple melodic parts combined according to counterpoint, as opposed to tonal music. Polyphonic music emphasizes the melodic nature of each part, creating contrast or complementarity between parts without a primary or secondary distinction.

In this long poem, Lu Jian creates a counterpoint between the main melody of the first stanza and the countermelody of the second stanza, allowing the themes of the poem to intersect and overlap, creating a duet-like "grand dialogue" of question and answer, singing and responding. In many large-scale musical works, the main melody is the primary theme, with the countermelody merely serving as a supplement. However, the countermelody of this long poem constantly challenges the main melody throughout each chapter, as if the poet deliberately uses external "non-poetic" elements to constantly exert pressure on the serious poetic theme, mocking or even desecrating the sublime with the mundane. The main melody at this point may be unaware of being, or perhaps has even forgotten its status as, the main melody, just as throughout the history of human civilization, at many periods, some kind of degenerate factor has dominated the world, quietly changing the course of world history.

In the second poem of Canto 20, "Poetry and the Times, Descending Scale," Lu Jian writes: "I stumble upon a poem, stumble upon a mood, such as/ in Nanxun Old Town of Huzhou, at Little Lotus Estate/.../ I look up at the Estate's name on an imposing plaque." "Within the gate what sways to the round of seasons?/ ...raising green canopies like at West Lake, and the pink beauty/ of flowers that go with the poetry of Yang Wanli/ I am like a Zhou Dynasty song collector, chanting 'Lotus leaves spread in fields.'"

As we know, the established poetic aesthetic tradition has formed an unwritten convention: stanzas (sections) with odd numbers of lines are unstable structures, while stanzas (sections) with even numbers of lines are stable structures. Based on this, Chinese and foreign poetry often uses four-line stanzas, as they are more conducive to expressing a complete and stable emotion and maintaining a sense of flow. Lu Jian, however, breaks with this poetic aesthetic convention and uses three-lined stanzas (i.e., odd-numbered sections). The poet's adoption of this consistent line structure stems primarily from the need to address the unstable mood of the entire poem: a mental state of free-fall and being on edge. Yet, viewed as a whole, it resembles a rigorous symphonic or operatic structure, or, more than that, a building that emphasizes symmetry and achieves balance within the instability of concepts similar to counterpoint—a majestic fusion of Chinese and Western elements.

Like a seasoned composer, Lu Jian skillfully employs polyphonic and fugal techniques, infusing the theme with various tonal and rhythmic variations, thus forming the poem's overarching theme and core image:

"poetry, life, and the poet." From a poetic aesthetic perspective, this technique, firstly, highlights the orderliness and integrity of the structure; secondly, it creates the counterpoint and echoing effects of polyphonic music; thirdly, it imparts the solemnity and splendor of religious music; and fourthly, it provides a cohesive, centripetal structure to a long poem that could easily have become disjointed.

3. Hybrid Linguistic Features

This long poem's experiments in textuality are both colorful and fruitful. Not only does it draw on the 2,000-year-old tradition of the "Fu, Bi, and Xing" (rhapsody, similitude, and framing image) from the *Book of Songs*, but it also experiments with a hybrid approach to poetic language from various angles and levels. This includes the interweaving and overlapping of symbolic language, surreal language, and key words (or word images), as well as the integration and blending of written and spoken language.

In this poem, Lu Jian, channeling Oscar Wilde, observes, "All the world's a stage, but the roles are miscast." His linguistic wit is glimpsed through his lines: "All the world's a stage, but the roles are miscast." His linguistic wit is glimpsed through these lines: "Today's great men are like the grasshopper caught/ under a straw hat thrown by a child..." "Greatness is but a wind blowing through the world; it is/ the simple yet sensitive heart, the desperate, leaf-like hands reaching/ holding back a maddened locomotive until the last moment." (Canto 19)

In the above lines, Lu Jian skillfully employs the metaphorical indicator "(just) like" to instantly bridge the spatial and psychological distance between the solemn terms and objects of "greatness" and "great people" and "children," "straw hats," "grasshoppers," and "the wind of the world." He then further extends the linguistic and figurative meanings of "greatness" and "great people" with the phrases "a simple yet sensitive heart" and "desperate leaf-like hands reaching." These lines employ metaphorical techniques while blending spoken and written language into seamless poetic lines.

For example, in the first stanza of Canto 15, "The Chinese Nation Is at Its Time of Greatest Danger," Lu Jian suddenly raises the theme of the poem (what one would call the leitmotif in music) by an octave: "In the most telling verse line of the past 100 years/ a nation is boiled down to the pivotal line of a poem/ it is '...at its time of greatest danger'// 'its time of greatest danger' is not about 1911/ it is not 1937 or 1946; it is not 1989/ It is today, this very day in front of our faces." "It is in the downfall of belief, the disarray of morals/ Even if a genius could create a brand new genre/ his precious fabric of words would only be taken for ravings." (Canto 15). Next, he extends the key phrase from the first stanza, its "time of greatest danger," into the final line of the first three stanzas of the second poem: "a nation is at its time of greatest danger." This not only echoes the title but also creates a parallel relationship between the upper and lower poems. He then re-embeds the phrase in the fifth stanza, creating a rhetorical repetition of the imagery of "greatest danger," blending seamlessly with the following lines: "...language would be a series of gasps/ rhymes would be garbage, queasily looping and oozing." The successful interweaving and overlapping of this key phrase (word image) within the poem not only strengthens the rhetorical function of the words but also deepens and elevates the poetic imagery.

Lu Jian is a true magician of language. He effortlessly and effortlessly writes about details of daily life, from food, love, childbirth, school, hospital, reading, socializing, and so on, to poetry creation, poetic language, and the current state of the poetry world. His long poem highlights the color, emotion, rhythm, and the sense of language and words themselves; it brings out contrast, balance and harmony between the long and short poems, and pays attention to the density of words and the structural combination of homophones, synonyms and antonyms, so that the language can penetrate into the texture of life and the cells of poetry, and ensure that the words and remain fresh, telling and appealing, so that the original power and keen penetration of words can be exerted to the maximum extent.

4. A witty and humorous style

Besides this, the witty and humorous style in Lu Jian's poetry is worth mentioning. For example, in the upper poem of Canto 25, "Science is Trial and Error, So is Life," he writes: "I once stumbled face down, repelled by a certain notion/ It was one forceful impulse, two wisps of emotion and three words/ an unspoken remark and a half-baked metaphor, seemingly fresh// yet drawing my blood. That innocent act felt like a crime/ The ambiguity of the sentence—almost betrayed me/ with traps of imagery and teetering discursive structure." (Canto 25).

He first describes how he once "stumbled," repelled by "a certain thought," then, in his heart, surged "an impulse, two strands of emotion, three words," a "remark," and "half-baked metaphor." But no one could imagine that such "impulses," "emotions," "words," and "remarks" would actually cause "me" to "bleed."

Let's look at Chapter 23 of the poem: "We poets are all minor figures/ By adding 'us' together we get/ one incomplete great poet. As for Borges// he has arrived with ease, we are on the road." The preceding statement says that "we" (small people), when added together, can only become an "incomplete great poet"; the following statement says that Borges "has arrived with ease," while we, surprisingly, are "still on the way."

In Canto 19, Lu Jian employs a self-deprecating tone, writing: "...the person I am this moment// is but a fragment of my life's duration/ My handful of poems are like ten uneven fingers/ all of them alike will eventually fall into the mud." This witty and humorous tone of his is found at every turn, another aspect of the poem's vividness, wit, and tension. Readers often cannot help but smile knowingly (Lu Jian's humorous style in poetry is also discussed in the first part of this article).

"My heart is filled with clouds and dreams, and the remaining space is vast and magnificent." (Su Shi, "On Visiting Biluo Cave, after the Rhyme of Cheng Zhengfu") Lu Jian is a scholar-poet who possesses a multifaceted artistic talent. In recent years, his poetry has consistently been eye-opening. He offers unique insights into poetic questions such as the nature of poetry, poetic language, and the relationship between poetry and life. If Lu Jian's successive releases of pan-narrative masterpieces since the turn of the century—"Dr. Leutete in the SARS Period" (June 2003), "34 Gifts" (May 2004), "Tianlou, Tianlou" (October 2006), "Bill on the Maple Leaf" (June 2006), "Sun on the Luo River" (April 2007), and "Steps in the Four Directions" (March 2008)—represent a series of sudden resurgences following a decade of silence following the simultaneous publication of his three poetry collections in 1992: "The Non-Existent Woman," "Famous Cities and Gates," and "The Geneva Sun." Afer that came Lu Jian's "Songs of a Resplendent Minor Poet," completed in September 2012, which represents a qualitative leap forward in the development of modern poetry. He creatively blends Dante's breadth of vision with Eliot's acumen and profoundness, presenting this classic long poem to be kept in the hallowed halls of Chinese poetry.

It should be pointed out that Lu Jian's poetic exploration was successful—especially this exquisite long poem, which approaches the realm of skilllessness. It is a masterpiece of contemporary Chinese long poetry and a model and representative work of the poetry of the New Narrative Period. It is precisely because of his unwavering commitment to poetry and his intellectual stance that Lu Jian, as a "watcher," tirelessly explored, forgetting food and sleep, and personally incorporating the artistic techniques and elements of the "Narration-related Verse" School into his entire poetic practice. This has led to a series of fruitful artistic projects, including intensive writing, a grassroots perspective (portraying the realities of contemporary peasants), the extensive use of humor, and the spiritual transplantation of classic poetry. In so doing he has presented us with a successful textual model for Chinese modern poetry and, beyond that, a "Lu Jian phenomenon."

March 17, 2013 in Guangzhou

Notes:

[1] "Poetry feature" refers to a new genre that uses poetry to reflect on social life by adapting the expressive technique of "close-ups" from film. Its characteristic is that it captures a characteristic aspect of a real-life person or event, depicting and portraying it in a focused, detailed, and striking manner, resulting in a high degree of authenticity and strong artistic appeal. This poetic genre was pioneered by Lu Jian.

Documentary poetry refers to a genre that faithfully portrays real people and events from real life or history in poetic form. Due to the inherent artistic and linguistic characteristics of poetry, documentary poetry is fundamentally different from documentary fiction, narrative poetry, and reportage. This author first uses the term "documentary poetry" to refer to Lu Jian's documentary poetry series. The above concept and definition are the author's original creation.

[2] The origin of the word "fugue" (German: fuge, French: fugue, Italian: fuga) varies, but is generally believed to derive from Latin, meaning "to chase" or "to fly." The main characteristic of a fugue is that the voices imitate each other, entering one another at different pitches and times.

Counterpoint forms corresponding phrases and images, creating an effect of question-and-answer chase between the parts. The art of fugue reached its peak from 16th-century religious music to the era of Bach in the 18th century.Counterpoint refers to the synthesis of two or more related but independent melodies into a single harmonic structure, while each melody maintains its own linear or horizontal melodic characteristics.

[3]Apollinaire (1880-1918), also known as "Guillaume Apollinaire," was the first and most celebrated French poet of the 20th century. He was a representative of Futurism and a forerunner of Surrealism. During his short life, he participated in all the avant-garde movements that dominated French literature and art in the early 20th century, leading poetry into unexplored territory and having a profound and far-reaching influence on modern poetry as a whole. Liu Mingjiu called Apollinaire "a courageous pioneer on the path of 20th-century poetry," "a figure whose talent, wisdom, acumen, pioneering spirit, and far-sighted theoretical vision guided the new trends in 20th-century poetry."

[4] The "Butterfly Effect" refers to the fact that in a dynamic system, a small change in initial conditions can trigger a long-term, massive chain reaction throughout the entire system. This concept has been developed theoretically in disciplines such as chaos theory, systems ecology, genetics, meteorology, logic, stock market theory, measure theory, functional analysis, topology, and fractal geometry.

[5] People with an acidic constitution have low blood calcium levels (the normal blood calcium level is 2.18-2.63 mmol/L; a level below this is considered calcium deficiency), which can lead to osteoporosis, a metabolic bone disease characterized by a decrease in the amount of bone tissue per unit volume.

[6] Also translated as "Bayard," Dante's spiritual lover and a character in his epic poem "The Divine Comedy." In the work, she rescues Dante from a ferocious beast, leads him out of the forest, and later travels with him to Paradise.

[7] The stapes, one of the three ossicles in the human ear, is shaped like a stirrup and connected to the incus bone. It is located in the middle ear cavity behind the eardrum, measuring only 2.6 to 3.4 mm and weighing only 2 to 4.3 mg.

[8] See "Poets on Poetry: American Poetry in the Mid-20th Century," page 244, Sanlian Bookstore, first edition, August 1989. In the American poetry world of that time, Beat poets often used their raging howls to expose the filth, chaos, and inhumanity of life. Confessional poets, on the other hand, exposed their personal lives, inner trauma, sexual desires, and even suicidal impulses with astonishing frankness. These two schools of poetry undoubtedly contributed to the trend toward more colloquial poetry.

[9] The "Narration-related Verse" School refers to a group of young poets active in the Chinese poetry scene in the 1980s and 1990s, converging in the early 1990s at the China New Poetry Institute (West Gate, No. 13, Xitao Hutong, Jiugulou Street, Beijing), and using poetry publications such as "Zhongwai Shixing" and "China Poets Newspaper" as their base. Representative poets include Qi Ren, Lu Jian, Ziwu (also known as Ni Nan, the founders of the group), Tian Yuan, Hong Zhu, Wang Mingyun, and Yan Zhi. In addition, a group of young literary figures who have come to Beijing to pursue their dreams, such as Shang Zhen, Pan Hongli, and Bei Ta, have maintained long-term, stable connections with the former through various means, both in poetry and in daily life, continuing to explore poetic issues and belonging to this school of poetry. (For details, see my article "The Origin and Artistic Aims of the Pan-Realistic School of Poetry," quoted from my book "On Pan-Realistic Poetry Poets," published by China Federation of Literary and Art Circles Press in 2013; or *Selected Poems of Contemporary Chinese Schools*, compiled by scholars from five countries, published by China Federation of Literary and Art Circles Press in August 2011.)

Ziwu ("Prime Meridian"), whose real name is Xu Yanliang, is a professional writer and literary critic at a literary research institute in Guangzhou, a cultural scholar, a member of the China Writers Association, the China Film Association, and the China Dramatists Association, and the artistic consultant for the multilingual edition of World Poets.

Lu Jian Afterword

Works That Can Destroy Their Authors
—Afterword to the Poetry Collection
"Songs of a Resplendent Minor Poet"

Lu Jian

What is the relationship between an author and his work? A mother-child relationship? "I" giving birth to another "I"? After the work is completed, does it reach the reader as an "independent entity," no longer connected to "I"? All are correct. So what is the relationship between them when the author is creating the work? A good work—only one good enough to touch the very core of humanity—is a relationship in which the work constantly hurts the author during the writing process.

My thinking on this question did not begin when I wrote "Songs of a Resplendent Minor Poet" (see *Zhongguo shige*, Issue 3, 2013), Perhaps because I'm slow-witted, I've pondered it for a long time. In the poem "Revisiting Cao Yu's Plays," written at the end of 1991, I argued that Cao Yu's art is "to snatch a handful of verses from our flesh and blood" (page 79 of my book "Famous Cities and Gates," published by Culture and Art Publishing House in September 1992). If the process of appreciation is like this, then creation should be even more so. "What use is this art/making me so obstinately focused? I've driven myself onto a road of no return because of it" (see my article "Confessing to Myself," "The Essence of a Century of Chinese Poetry," People's Literature Publishing House, May 2002, p. 528). This means that I was able to express something "my own" only when I was on the verge of a "dead end" in life. Regarding Vincent van Gogh, in August 1991, in "Hurried

Sunflowers" (see *October* magazine, issue 3, 1995, and "The Geneva Sun," October 1992, Taiwan Shizhihua Publishing House, p. 34), I wrote, "My pain surges boundlessly/Genius is a human disease." A key purpose of artistic talent is to reach the limit of feeling others' pain and joy, and to find ways to express them through familiar means. If one inadvertently pushes beyond this limit, one will go mad. I can still vividly recall the feeling of internal heat attacking my heart and blood choking my throat as I wrote this poem. Van Gogh must have felt even worse when painting in Arles, France. Similarly, Boris Pasternak, the author of Doctor Zhivago, and George Orwell, author of 1984, experienced such a fate. Goethe spent sixty years tormented by the writing of Faust. Chen Zhongshi was consumed by the novel *White Deer Plain*, to the point of never writing a major work again. Cao Xueqin's struggle with *Dream of the Red Chamber* brought on serious illness, but *Dream of the Red Chamber* ultimately prevailed—the author died of exhaustion before it was even finished. Gao E revived the novel, but it was too late for Cao Xueqin. Liang Shanbo and Zhu Yingtai, for example, used real-life performance to make their unprecedented love story come true. The romantic poet Haizi, who "walked to the end of humanity" by the secluded path of poetry, committed suicide at Shanhaiguan. Such examples abound; this is fate, "Fate's size is our size" (see "Turn over the Cards of Fate" in Chapter M of "Songs of a Resplendent Minor Poet"). Some writers, like Jia Pingwa after *Wasted City* and Mo Yan after *The Sandalwood Death*, survived despite the hurt they endured. It's not that their spirits possess a remarkable capacity for self-recovery, but rather that these works are not the type that is written at the cost of one's life. They do not reach the level of greatness that is extracted from a writer's very bones. Great works lie in anticipation and in the unknown. The entire history of literature and art is a history of writers and artists whose lives drained away.

Almost every work that touches the deepest depths of the reader's soul, profoundly reflecting the essence of human existence, has a certain devastating effect on the creator. The author releases, consumes, exhausts, bleeds, collapses, their brain plundered, their brain wrung out, their spirit weightless, uncertain if they still have strength or value. To write the next book, they must start all over again—accumulating knowledge and experience, summoning up intelligence and skills. Masters become alienated from their own lives, as if their very lives have been reset to zero. Why?

These works open a secret passage, offering a glimpse into the mysteries of existence. These mysteries are invisible to the naked eye, almost invariably afflicted by cataracts. These mysteries are close to divine secrets: as the ancient Chinese said, "Heaven's secrets must not be revealed." Eyes that behold the glare of truth are bound to be wounded. "Heaven is jealous of a talented person" is not about jealousy, for nothing within human reach is worthy of envy. God thwarts him unintentionally, without extra effort. God may be a vast black hole; by connecting with Him you may tap into its energy, but your own energy is also being sucked away. I've always had a vague feeling that artists are more likely to offend God than scientists. Within God's vast scale, scientists perceive the scales of reality with specificity, yet God has the overall view. Artists suffer and agonize while a ball of fire or obscuring mist hovers overhead. Sometimes, God doesn't know what he's doing—it seems human folly isn't so simple—and it annoys him, ultimately imposing a price on human "artists." Shakyamuni attained Buddhahood at the cost of obscuring Prince Suddhodana. God created humanity, and though he lived, he could only sacrifice his own son to allow others to understand his vast inner being. Does creation by human artists come easily? Do they have priority over the gods in influencing others?

Perhaps these considerations are delusional and unfounded. "When humans think, God laughs." This is because human contemplation of God is like a group of ants discussing the galaxy. But contemplating human matters doesn't necessarily make God laugh. If humans refuse to even consider their own affairs, isn't that unforgivable laziness? Thus, scientists and artists exhaust their energies, vie to demonstrate their intelligence, joyfully or dejectedly exploring existential issues, describing the world, and expressing their own pain and joy. In this way, scientists and artists emerge.

Here, I should cite the writing of "Songs of a Resplendent Minor Poet" as an example. Clearly, it's not a work imbued with divine power, but rather one steeped in the mundane. It addresses the question, "What is the role of a poet in this world?" As we know, poetry isn't always used as a means of resolving specific issues. Qu Yuan's "Heavenly Questions" merely raises questions. "Songs of a Minor Poet" gazes up at the heavens, looks down at the earth, and surveys the vastness of my surroundings, attempting to live and write as I wish. "Even if a genius could create a brand new genre/ his precious fabric of words could only be flawed." ("The Sword Hanging High," canto O, "Songs of a Minor Poet"). He understands this, yet he refuses to resign himself. He seeks to achieve "resplendence"—to borrow a Chinese term from architecture—the best state within his capabilities. However, he suffers from numerous illnesses and endless troubles, embracing the flaws of both traditional literati and modern poets. Now, he must reckon with himself, expose himself to the sun, and discern his true pathologies. He faces countless challenges: human frailty, a subjective perspective that blinds him to the truth, a value orientation that worries about gain and loss, the vanity of worldly success, weakness, laziness, a lack of faith and responsibility, and a tendency to drift with the tide. The relationship between him, his poetry, and the outside world encompasses questions of faith, the integration of Chinese and Western cultural traditions, the relationship between self and society, the chaotic world and the possibility of salvation, the poet's relationship with poetry, and with language. The threads are numerous and difficult to unravel. This is why a poem of just over 700 lines consumed nearly six years of my life. I was determined to exchange six years of my life for a single poem, but since "a precious fabric of words would be taken for ravings," could this poem have had a different ending?

I think the author of "Songs of a Resplendent Minor Poet" is at least honest. This is specifically reflected in the following: First, we stand at a point in history—a point on the vertical axis of time. Our predecessors are towering, and everything we have today is connected to them. They have never left us; whenever we think of them, they appear. They still draw upon our minds and bodies, and their erstwhile thoughts and expressions have already outstripped us. "Songs of a Minor Poet" not only draws nourishment from their thoughts but also builds on their words, attempting to offer a "unique poetic text reflecting the artist's present state." In this poem, through quotations, these predecessors seem united, forming a stable formal structure for "Songs of a Minor Poet." All of this reinforces the author's confidence, believing that this poetic journey has benefited from the help of those who came before, and that this writing exercise will be a rewarding endeavor (though it involves trial and error) that surely will have something to show for itself. At the same time, the predecessors erected a formidable barrier for the author, forcing him to speak to them at eye level, for his ambition was to "pick up where the predecessors left off" (see "Neither a Brush nor a Quill" in Canto C of "Songs of a Minor Poet"). This is a high bar for any contemporary poet. From a macroscopic perspective, poetry is not the sole achievement of an individual; rather, all people, past and present, are writing a shared opus about humanity, and all individual talents, efforts, and products are insignificant. The author of "Songs of a Minor Poet" is well aware of this, and thus his stance, or rather, his position within the poem, is neither less than that of any predecessor, nor above that of the "snickering girl on the street corner." He is present—he reflects on the predecessors' intentions, feels the world and himself, and speaks—creating a discourse field based on his location, thoughts, and feelings. Secondly, to pay tribute to the predecessors and to express sincerity to the readers, the specific people and events mentioned in "Songs of a Minor Poet" are almost all real. Regarding the general rules of poetic composition, aside from epics and poetic reports with a strong documentary nature, the factuality of the characters and events depicted is unimportant. However, "Songs of a Minor Poet" deliberately adheres to the principle of authenticity, encompassing the author's social career, family, and emotional life. These are the foundation and elements of his "personal epic." In describing his real experiences and life, in the context of "presence," the author's emotions are more fully realized. This authenticity enables the poet to bow to no social force or individual, and to shed tears in the face of the wind without shame. A cautious "silence," the refined elegance of a "gentleman," and the illusory pursuit of honor are all out of the question. He shows no favoritism to anyone (including himself), never concealing the honorable and the virtuous. Praise and criticism are determined by the individual. Thirdly, the poetic language is mixed. "Songs of a Minor Poet" contains classical Chinese (primarily in the quotations), written language, and spoken language. The quality of a poem is not directly related to its register of language; it must be determined by the needs of the poem itself. As for "Songs of a Minor Poet," it requires a strong stomach. We are confronted with the entirety of humanity's past spiritual achievements, the entirety of today's chaotic world and China's savage reality, as well as the poet's own shattered life. The semantics are mixed, the grammar is chaotic, and these things crowd the poet's mind. If speech is poetry, it would be surprising if it weren't a mixture of mud and sand. Therefore, this mixed state must be a deliberate act of the author's adherence to the principle of "truth," including the occasional outburst of expletives—giving the appropriate verbal response to things that deserve expletives.

I strongly adhere to Mr. Shan Zhansheng's division of my own creative periods in his article "The Mental Journey of Lu Jian's Poetry." I'd even consider all my writing prior to "Songs of a Resplendent Minor Poet" to be a "practice period." Shan Zhansheng says that before this, "Lu Jian's understanding of man, society, and the universe was still separate: man was man, and the world was the world. But with "Songs of a Resplendent Minor Poet," man and the world are no longer separate; man is the whole of the world." While many critics have accorded considerable recognition and attention to Lu Jian's poetry collections, such as "Famous Cities and Gates" and "The Geneva Sun" from the early 1990s and "Warmth" from the early 2000s, even "Songs of a Resplendent Minor Poet" has its share of differing opinions. For example, a poetry editor at a prominent publication expressed his dislike, calling it a typical "intellectual writing" with all the hallmarks of that camp. "Who writes poetry like that anymore?" One netizen commented that he'd rather read chaotic poetry than poetry that old women could recite. I've always had doubts about the concept of "intellectual writing." I believe writing shouldn't overemphasize knowledge and so-called wisdom. Poetry can't be composed solely with the mind; it must involve the whole body. Writing should also be challenging, and large-scale works must have a corresponding overall design and formal structure. I have certainly made my share of attempts to deconstruct realities and employ colloquial language, such as "Twenty-first-century morality has lost its lofty mountaintop grandeur. Tradition is like an old ship, its deck and oars shattered. Set it on fire, and then cool the last samovar. Discourse is a circle formed by the public's collars. Sewn around a frequently replaced mouthwash cup. Far from shore, the past is hard to recapture. Our happy life has been dragged down like this. // You're white, I'm white; you're black, we're black; no one should criticize anyone. You pull, I push; you fill, we pile; no one should blame anyone. Officials, civilians, and bandits refer to the old society. God has fallen, the law is a crime; it's a postmodern aesthetic. Empty talk, no profit, no loss, shame, shame. Our happy life is me dragging you down. You drag me down, we drag everyone down. Everyone drags us all down" (my humble work, "Our Happy Life," published in the December 2005 issue of *Xingxing Poetry Magazine*). This shows that I am who I am, and I don't want to "be anyone" or "be like anyone." Is this why all the poetic trends and schools have nothing to do with me? Szymborska said that if writing poetry is boring, then "between the boredom of writing poetry and the boredom of not writing poetry, I still choose the former." Life is painful, and between the pain of writing poetry and the pain of not writing poetry, I also choose the former. I am an apprentice of poetry, willingly accepting its blows. My ideal is to spend my lifetime "swapping sheaves of poems at gatherings of insignificant verses" (see "Compline Prayer" in "Songs of a Minor Poet"), gently picked up and put down by the hand of time. "There are only poems in this world, no poets" (see "I thought of it, but didn't do it, and I still think" in "Songs of a Minor Poet"). Our so-called "talent" is not that important. In fact, whether we have talent or not is not certain.

April 1, 2013, Beijing

(Originally published in the poetry collection "Songs of a Resplendent Minor Poet," published by Tomorrow Publishing House in December 2013)

About Lu Jian

Lu Jian, whose ancestral home is Fufeng, Shaanxi Province, was born in Cangzhou, Hebei Province in 1956. He completed primary and secondary school in Luoyang, Henan Province, and spent four and a half years working in the countryside in Nanyang. In 1978, he was admitted to the Beijing Broadcasting Institute. He has worked at China Central Radio and the Henan Provincial Federation of Literary and Art Circles. He is currently a retired professor at the Communication University of China. He joined the China Writers Association in 1991.

Major publications:

Poetry collection "Prayers Beneath the Red Cross," May 1989, Haiyan Publishing House

Poetry collection "The Loud Voice at the Window," November 1990, Singapore Cultural and Academic Association

Poetry collection "Beautiful Windy Night" (co-authored with Yi Dianxuan), March 1991, Huashan Literature and Art Publishing House

Poetry collection "The Non-Existent Woman," August 1992, Hong Kong Jinling Publishing Company

Poetry collection "Famous Cities and Gates," September 1992, Cultural and Art Publishing House

Poetry collection "The Sun in Geneva," 199 October 2002, Taiwan Shizhihua Publishing House

Poetry Collection "Selected Poems of Lu Jian", October 1998, China Federation of Literary and Art Circles Publishing House

Poetry Collection "Dr. Lele Tete During the SARS Period", June 2003, Spring Breeze Literature and Art Publishing House

Literary Criticism Collection "101 Famous Foreign Short Poems of the 20th

Century: An Appreciation", July 2003, Zhuhai Publishing House

Poetry Collection "34 Gifts", May 2004, Beijing Broadcasting Institute Press

Poetry Collection "Seven Discourses", November 2005, Shenyang Publishing House

Poetry Collection "Maple Leaf" Bill on the Mountain, August 2006, Shenzhen Haitian Publishing House

Poetry Collection "Mosaic Puzzle," September 2006, Writers Publishing House

Poetry Collection "Tianlou, Tianlou," October 2006, Zhongzhou Ancient Books Publishing House

Poetry Collection "On the Yang of the Luo River," April 2007, Henan Literature and Art Publishing House

Literary Criticism Collection "Images, Images," November 2007, Shaanxi People's Publishing House

Poetry Collection "Four-Sided Steps," March 2008, Hong Kong Art Market Publishing House

Poetry Collection "Warmth," December 2008 Liaoning People's Publishing House

Poetry Collection "Songs of a Resplendent Minor Poet," December 2013, Tomorrow Publishing House

Poetry Collection "Some Fragments," June 2014, China Radio and Television Publishing House

Poetry Collection "N Old Man in the Poetry World," November 2014, Xianzhuang Bookstore

Poetry Collection "Thoughts Arise," December 2017, Henan Literature and Art Publishing House

Poetry Collection "On the Sun of the Luo River" (Revised Edition), January 2021, Zhengzhou University Press

Poetry Collection "Opening: Selected Poems of 2020," July 2021, Zhengzhou

University Press Publisher

Poetry Collection "Short and Long" December 2022, China Poetry, Calligraphy and Painting Publishing House

Poetry Collection "Selected Poems of Lu Jianchang" December 2023, China Poetry, Calligraphy and Painting Publishing House

Poetry Collection "Selected Poems of Lu Jianchang on Foreign Themes" December 2023, China Poetry, Calligraphy and Painting Publishing House

Poetry Collection "South of the North, North of the South" December 2023, Baihuazhou Literature and Art Publishing House

Poetry Collection "I Call It Light" August 2024, Liaoning People's Publishing House

Awards:

Poetry Collection "Yearning for the Sea" won the "Feitian" Award in 1982

The poem "In the Sky, on the Shore, in the Water" won the first Outstanding Work Award from the Poetry God magazine in 1985.

The poem "Three Soldiers and Their Beards" won the 1985 Star Poetry Award.

The poem "Hurried Sunflowers" won the 1995 October Literature Award.

The poem cycle "Stories of the 20th Century" won the 1999 People's Literature Annual Award.

The poem cycle "Poetry N Old Man" won the first Dahe Editor-in-Chief Poetry Award from Dahe Poetry magazine in 2011.

The poem cycle "Is Mother In 2013, his poem "Songs of a Resplendent Minor Poet" won the first "China (Wencheng) Liu Bowen Poetry Award" from Poetry Magazine.

In 2013, his poem "Warm Snow and the Poems Before It" won third prize in the third "Guo Moruo Poetry Award" from China Writers Association.

In 2014, his long poem "Songs of a Resplendent Minor Poet" won the first "China Qu Yuan Poetry Award" from the Chinese Poetry Society.

In 2014, his poetry collection "Songs of a Resplendent Minor Poet" won first prize in the first "China Ruan Zhangjing Poetry Award" from Guangdong Province.

"Songs of a Resplendent Minor Poet" won the First China (Foshan) Long Poetry Award in 2014.

The poetry collection "Songs of a Resplendent Minor Poet" won the Second Chang Yao Poetry Award in 2018.

The long poem "Sick Wife" won the "China 30 Years Outstanding Long Poet Award" from Poetry Reference in 2019.

Collections of Research Papers on Lu Jian's Poetry

"About a Poet" by Xiaoxue, Zhang Tongwu, Lu Jian, et al., published by Baihua Literature and Art Publishing House in February 1997.

"Poems, a Tribute to Classics" published by Xianzhuang Bookstore in April 2014.

Denis Mair: Brief bio

Denis Mair holds an M.A. in Chinese from Ohio State University and has taught as lecturer at Whitman College and University of Pennsylvania. He was research fellow for many years at Hanching Academy (Sun Moon Lake), worked as translation consultant for Zhongkun Cultural Fund, Beijing, and served as translator for Jidi Majia (Deputy Chair, Chinese Writers Association). Denis translated books by the Buddhist monk Shih Chen-hua (SUNY Albany, 1992), the philosopher Feng Youlan (Hawaii University, 2000), and the art critic Zhu Zhu (Hunan Fine Arts, 2009). His poetry translations include: *Frontier Taiwan* (Columbia University Press, 2005); *Contemporary Chinese Poetry* (Shanghai Literary Arts, 2007); Yan Zhi, *Reading the Times* (Homa & Sekey, 2012); Jidi Majia, *Rhapsody in Black* (Univ. of Oklahoma, 2014); Jidi Majia, *Shade of Our Mountain Range* (Mkhiva Foundation, 2014); Luo Ying, *Memories of the Cultural Revolution* (Univ. of Oklahoma, 2015); Jidi Majia, *From the Snow Leopard to Mayakovsky* (Kallatumba Press, 2017); Yang Ke, *Two Halves of the World Apple* (Univ. of Oklahoma, 2017), as well as *7+2 Mountain Climber's Journal* (White Pine, 2020). He has also translated poetry by Yan Li, Meng Lang and many others. His own poetry collection *Man Cut in Wood* was published by Valley Contemporary Poets (Los Angeles, 2004).

诗 歌 篇

1. 我对自己说吉约姆是你来的时候了

——（法）吉约姆·阿波利奈

A. 阿波利奈能来我当然也能

我的天职是塑造一个当代诗人的形象
我必须千百次地打碎、塑造我自己
古往今来来过无数人，他们中的

许多人自从来了，再也没有消失过
他们哭、笑、得意、痛不欲生，曾经
忧虑或嘲笑我们。他们是我们的亲人

又与我们毫无关系。他们高大伟岸
有时又会从我们的指缝间漏走
他们用话语堵住我们的嘴巴

a. "我"的含义

我就是我，不是昨天的我
不是未来的我，不是一个
概念、定义，是一个肉身

说我长着一个铁制的头颅
木制的躯干与双手，泥坯
堆成的腿脚，我惊讶，我反对

我有着亚洲人的正常体魄
除了心肠有点软，浑身上下
硬梆梆的，生殖力旺盛

我的主食是面粉、稻谷、玉米
儒家和道家的笔墨。通过翻译
品尝面包和西方文化的滋味

我是农耕文明的产物，被机器
快速裹挟，一头扎进计算机里
小心翼翼，护住自己的软肋

在他人面前把我的优点尽量放大
我是暴政的敌人，同时又是
一个温良的托尔斯泰主义者

2. 我是无名之辈，你是谁？

——（美）狄金森

B. 桂冠

其实唐朝，李白还是李黑，又有
什么区别呢？高行健是法国人
还是中国人，又有什么关系呢？

当年诺贝尔创立他的奖项
就因为这全都没关系。两千年来
人们写的文字，全是一部作品

一顶桂冠从一个荷马头上，转移到
另一个荷马头上。他自己是看不见这
桂冠的，他看见的是自己内心的黑暗

b. 我是谁更好些？

我的上嘴唇掀动，说，跟我没关系
下嘴唇紧接着就予以否定
我是谁更好些？我要看到现世报

如果像狄金森那样就干脆不写
我当个特级厨师，烤火鸡
烤得外焦里嫩卖个好价钱

人忙碌一生，当国家主席也是忙
作鞋匠也是忙。不如忙出点道道来
我从小信奉的是这种哲学

耶稣手持宽容，我不清楚
自己是否在宽容的屋檐下面
他的仁慈是否也照耀古老的东方

我知道自己在做什么，我不知道
自己在做什么。周易，周——
圆周的周，万物轮回周而复始

我忽而巨大忽而渺小，少不经事
四十而惑，五十不知天命，活着
活着就把自己活成了这个样子

3. 读书破万卷，下笔如有神

——（中）杜甫

C. 不是毛笔，也不是鹅毛笔

我的左手握住诗歌，右手抓住现实
用音乐对位法和图象法写诗
常常类乎抄袭，偶尔灵光闪现

在前贤止步的地方起笔
从波德莱尔以来便是如此
我知道自己仍然是个小人物

儿时为长大而吃饱穿暖；然后下身
与智力一同胀大。饱读杂书，用
手指和键盘的相互取悦代替书写

c. 我们这个时代的诗人

老杜有老杜的途径，顾城有顾城的绝招
就像练球，下笔时得有人给喂球
所以，杜甫的落点总在古典主义界内

我看你时很远，我看云时很近。暗示
要精选题材，先外后内先远后近
别人懵了，我就贴近了给自己的定位

我们这个时代的诗人，脖子长的
叫小 a 小 b 小 c 小 d，脖子短些的
叫阿猫阿狗小鱼小虾。开始我们

光着屁股，整天一起打闹，后来
变声期时，一下子奔逃四散
谁也叫不出别人的名字。但是从此

奇怪的事情频频发生，我在最痛苦或
最欢乐的时候，大叫一声，总听见
别人在答应。有人说西川心里有一个

肥壮的于坚，怎么会呢？有人说
于坚心里倒置着一个西川，那是污蔑
说他们有点嫉妒对方，却是不无可能

4. 她恍若上界的一位天使，降临人间把奇迹向我们显示

—— （意）但丁

D. 但丁和扑克牌

但丁站在"A"字之尖顶上，俯视人类
的生路和死路；我站在"V"字的谷底
沉溺于深渊，向左边和右边呼救

我们的自赎像莱茵河畔哥特式
城堡里骑士们在壁炉旁打牌
你叫一张里尔克，他甩一张德里达

维特根斯坦暂时在小 b 的手里占了上风
中国的太阳隔一层魔障，我们不小心就
喜欢上了肯德基和家乐福的购物卡

d. 香蕉人居室和皱眉头的大师

有人说我故作严肃，作外国名士状
居室中到处张贴欧美名家语录
在大师的肩膀后面窥视世界

有人在我的作品里常常遇到熟人
因此不得不常常脱帽致敬。有人说
我面无表情，用脖子举着自己的画像

招摇过市。在汉语中夹杂拼音文字
我先天不足，不得不如此
抱歉，一会儿詹姆斯先生光临寒舍

有人说不仅诗人如此，小说家更甚
作品的大小尺寸全是量身订做
比如把《老人与海》的标点符号

先抄下来，然后往里面填满汉字
让马悦然先生读的摸不着头脑
击节叫好，评奖时投下关键的一票

谁说的，诗歌是翻译漏掉的部分
诱导译者锦上添花是最大的学问？
抱歉，詹姆斯先生已经在敲门

5. 他们急忙摘下一些无花果叶盖住身体

—— （古希伯来《旧约全书》）

E. 树叶和果实

人类在伊甸园中获得的第一个权利
是隐私权。亚当和夏娃，用树叶
遮住身体。人们反文化，就先反这个

人们研究文化，就频频意淫
成人保健用品呼啸在乡镇，网站
裸聊，夏装露出脐部及两瓣后臀

女人的裙子越来越短，成为美感
科学技术的聪明发明了冰箱
它要为陈旧的故事保持新鲜

e. 一首诗能引导我们走多远

一首诗能引导我们走多远。或者
说，我们距离一首诗多远。等等
我忘了回一位美女的电话

来电：3.1415926，八位数，显然
是一个大城市打来的。留言简洁
不勉强人，想必有着良好的教养

诗歌可以带我们去往任何地方
但我们的生命是她的口粮
因为对真实的排斥只好把她压低

我们从村庄里出来，要找什么
自己也不大知道。反正要吃饭
最好吃好点；反正要穿衣

最好是名牌；我们要搞女人
应该搞一个漂亮的或者让一个
漂亮的来搞。那就先搞诗歌吧

在彻底的唯物主义者面前
精神只有被强奸的份。有人拍手
既是命中劫数，我权当甜点来享受

6. 文章合为时而著，歌诗合为事而作

——（中）白居易

F. 谁已为我而死？我将为谁而死？

鲁班已为比尔·盖茨而死；苏东坡
已为黄庭坚而死；博尔赫斯已为光明
失去了他那有洞察力的眼睛

士兵已为将军而死，生命已为棺木而死
成就生不生锈不得而知，反正历史
要判断，词语要擦拭。生活。写作

比做爱更用力，比用力更使劲
纵使世界已被拼贴成一张扁平的脸
诗人注定是那个挺身而出的鼻子

f. 微博时代的写作

我的电脑竟然敲不出这两个字
——微博，它宁肯在别人那里
在大街上。公交车上的少女

低头坐在那儿，不停发消息
昨天一位朋友她说，要夹你了
我赶紧回：是"加"不是"夹"

"从明天开始，我也是诗人了"
"我毫不怀疑"。其实我心不在焉
正在回忆下午饭前的场景——

朋友介绍：这是位诗人。官员
一粗一细的眉毛抖动了一下；老板
一高一低的嘴角略微上扬。我

肚子里咕噜着一股浩然正气
差点泄露出去，却比平时
更绅士更僵硬地点头。哦诗歌

过去道德的上帝盯上了她
如今商品的上帝要主宰她
诗歌为我们受尽凌迟之苦

7. 在雅典娜的帮助下，

阿喀琉斯一挥长矛正中赫克托尔的颈项

——（古希腊）荷马

G. 阿喀琉斯的长矛借助了荷马的膂力

文字和人类一样，需要放血疗法
诗歌的斧头砍上去，它流血
它流血的同时我倒下，借助灰土的传扬

阿喀琉斯一挥长矛，杀了赫克托尔
二次大战的扫帚一抡，人类肃然
爱因斯坦使太空的道理弯曲

意识形态螺旋上升，民族、国家、主义
流派和诗歌的本质、原则、手法。我的
手掌上的纹理，也是假借了自由的名义

g. 一代人能解决一个多大的问题

我吃了一千碗饭，为伦勃朗的绘画
镶上一幅铝合金的画框；我洗了

一百次澡，濡湿黄宾虹的狼毫

在他的山水间添上一抹亮色
八大山人的鸟鸣刚被听见
艾略特就在他的黄昏里昏过去了

博尔特比鲍威尔提高了0、16秒
哲学家回过头去研究老子的高妙
我的书案摊开《道德经》17个版本

时间的吊臂摆动，也许历史在前
未来在后，也许是它的反面
也许我穷尽一生完成一个错误

我的光源是60瓦白炽灯我的眼睛
是30瓦的视力。呕是谁的电话
我的深夜恰好没存这个号码

女友照例扬颈吞下一粒丸药
她把收拾床铺的声音弄得很响
还把暧昧的眼神朝我传递

8. 我悲哀地看着我们这一代人

——（俄）莱蒙托夫

H. 我们这一代人悲哀地看着莱蒙托夫

学术秀、真人秀、做秀、模仿秀
口齿伶俐秀、结结巴巴秀。作
沉思状、作假想状荒诞状、作

左半身右半身极不对称状
装嫩、装酷、装相、装死狗
你扎它一下，它就逾墙走

我被襁褓生出来而非从母体出世
我的智慧来自真理而非来自生活
我们这一代人悲哀地看着莱蒙托夫

h. 迅速成名的葵花宝典

甲、给自己起一个别致的笔名
假如一位上海诗人，最好叫外白
与他唱和的女友恰如其分地名叫渡桥

乙、借助名校，把诗歌运动起来
热热闹闹，自己的名字活色生香
出现在大刊小报及各种选本之中

丙、官方民间两不得罪。诗坛已呈颓势
在污染物与杂草之间穿行，将来做大时
再以春秋笔法进行外科手术式的批评

丁、学外语。说得跟跟跄跄没关系
写诗清一色欧式句子，便于翻译
最好找李笠直接捎到斯德哥尔摩去

戊、站在煊赫有力的魁梧身形旁边
人们在看见他们的同时看见了我
在看见刺绣品的同时看到了针线

己、作死了个别名人的对立面
当然以无辜者的面目出现。而且
胆大包天的成功者心是比针尖还细的

9. 苟余心之端直兮，虽僻远其何伤?

——（中）屈原

I. 当代的美快步而行

在他的歌唱中楚国、怀王都成为美
死成为美。极端事物无不有美潜隐
其中，刀剑的锋芒，灰姑娘的脚

维纳斯断臂的边缘。一张俏丽的脸
等待着去掉雀斑；一匹跛马被医成
宝马，口疮和口吃同时不再流行

但花朵已无力保护它的花香，罂粟的美
决定了她必须躲躲藏藏，长髯飘飘的
拉琴者最后拉断了自己的脖子

i. 语言的扮相

总觉得《诗经》《橘颂》的作者
在嘲讽今日的写家。其实《诗经》作者
没功夫挑刺，他们只是钟爱名词

至唐代诗人——文采风流，像一群
勤快的丫鬟给小姐梳头，刮腻子擦粉
用形容词把诗歌的品相打磨装修

细致到几乎遭小姐烦的程度。后世
的才子们似乎得到要领，当仁不让
拼命给语言吃糖，把名词牙蛀掉

甚至给笔下的事物隆胸，嫁接、拼凑
生造、割裂概念，如同超市的
"火烧冰激凌"；比如国与家这

两个词汇，从泾渭分明到模糊不清
比如道和理，竟成了同性恋关系
伊人在水一方，如今滚成一团

我听见房东捂嘴窃笑，我看见
贾似道，当年朝服下面隐隐
露出的两只脚，各穿一种鞋子

10. 生存在你所生存的地方

—— （瑞典）古尔贝里

J. 不在昌平，不在西宁

不是昌耀，不是海子，不在昌平的小屋
不在罗布麻的青海湖旁，北京同样
需要有人站岗，看穿世界的心肠

就在我脚心下面，下盘需要定力
我伸出手来，是要索取，还是
送给别人他所需要的东西？

在闪念间，在被虫子蠹空的日历里
在籍，在册，在人群中蹩蹀而行
捏着一支粉笔，我在定福庄东街一号

j. 我的蛮横的爱和生活的具体

我的蛮横的爱和生活的具体
要求我不能把自己的孤单灌醉
然后发出庞大的呓语

我眼观工资条：一是一二是二
我周边，缺少阔大而粗砺的自然
海子的版图及抱负对我也无眷顾

我的原则：不接着别人的话
往下说，假如不便当面反驳
就把眼神放到窗户外面或眼皮下面

不主动帮老板赚钱，即便是
仅仅"出卖荒凉"的老板
荒凉在我眼里，还没出道的勇士一般

我多想天苍苍野茫茫，活个洒脱通透
可是儿子太小，春天太瘦
我紧拽她褴褛的衣袖——用我赶去

上班时握紧自行车把的手，我的把
一个女人从少女拥抱成半老徐娘的手
可是这又怎能成为我妥协的借口？

11. 每个人都应该对世上一切人和一切事物负责

—— （俄）陀思妥耶夫斯基

K. 免责，不免责

有人对一切人一切事负责，就是不对
自己负责；有人不对一切负责除了自我
上午我挂号之后，医生要我对肚子里

莫须有的囊肿负责，而他只对医院
的收费处负责。黄昏的公园角落里她
抽抽搭搭地，恋爱已经无法向处女负责

就像诗人应该向字、词的皮癣负责
语言的脾胃不适，它摄取的营养单一
以致骨质疏松，体质时常虚弱

k. 诗歌的"有用之用"

人的名字，花的称谓，"黄鹤楼"烧酒
"一片云"牌湿巾、"司机一滴酒，
亲人两行泪"的标语；一个水壶

壶嘴被设计成樱桃小口的模样
一个皮包，它的翻盖和铜扣
像精致的五官；长安街边的

某座大楼我们用"裤衩子"
来形容其外貌；用"屁股指挥大脑"
概括某国令人哭笑不得的当代政治

现在连卫生巾都已经梦想诗味了
绵延数公里的香榭丽舍大街整个
像一条叮当作响的花花肠子

可是又有谁会认为春节和圣诞节
不是两出精彩难分高下的诗剧？
以及水墨，油彩；象棋与国际象棋

诗歌的有用之用，投射在我们面前
的影像上，缤纷，纷繁。它有时是
文字，有时是一份猝不及防的礼物

12. 吾所以有大患者，为吾有身

——（中）老子

L. 大患吾身与大美吾身

世界什么都不缺，我们空空如也
春光没有在我们的身体里居住
我们也不知道自己是谁

我有一个接受的入口，一个排泄的
出口，而具人形；简陋居室
粗茶淡饭和大把药片，和一个姓名

想象自己成为一只鹰，凌空；成为
一枝花啜饮露水，殷殷笑意地
感恩大地，而不得

l. 一个孱弱的精子是我的前身

一个孱弱的精子是我的前身
我父亲在生我之前已经残废
留给我唯一的遗产就是原罪

我主要的培养基：母亲、舅舅、姨父
小知识分子、右派专家、公私合营
对象，他们默默一生无声响

我重要的营养液：大跃进、反右倾
三年自然灾害、文革十年风起云涌
以大有作为名义作一粒乡下的害虫

睁着饿得发绿、瞳孔放大的双眼
我惧怕所有人，仇视一切人
在梦遗里忙于亵渎美丽的女性

若不是又有了书读，我早就成了
天牢囚徒、梁山毛贼，五脏六腑
把那一带的好人好事全消化干净

岂是几杯水酒能够醉倒？岂是
些许招安可以软化？笑里藏刀
我细瘦的书生之手，也能见血封喉

13. 写作要选取适合自己的题材

——（古罗马）贺拉斯

M. 掀开命运的纸牌

翻开题材这个词语，看到故事
挑开事件，看到我们的人生
我们苍茫、苍白或仓皇的人生

这是被命运指定的内容，因此
我们时而被自己或别人的笔触感动
命运，它的大小就是我们的大小

我们写其它东西全是无用功
我们已有的其它写作，无论如何勤勉
除了练笔功能，全是无效劳动

m. 医院病房中斜斜的光线

当时，朋友只剩下病历上的时光
愤懑，他的床位在逼仄的门后
二人无言久坐，他送我下楼

半月后我送他去一个有烟囱的
院落；半月后我染疾躺卧，护士
拉开窗帘，病房照进斜斜的光线

我想，我从来没有不是个病人
在家中解决口腹之欲，性欲
高兴时是傻子，痛苦时是诗人

执起教鞭把知识的营养与毒素
均匀搅拌，灌进学生食道，换回
我的柴米油盐和深深的愧疚

多么平凡？却又惊心动魄！我
想起自己有意或无意给别人的
伤害，他们不是我的病友

就是我的亲人。在命运面前
我除了不配合、反抗，还有悔恨
有刹车的声音，有加油的声音

14. 爱的欢乐只能用艺术的形式来表达

——（印）泰戈尔

N. 人类最有价值的创造

能够包围一座城池的，是爱
能够包围整个地球的，只能是爱
这是我们看到的、体验到的

创造的，能够作比的唯有空气和水
像裸露的珍宝随处可见，普通
普遍，像耶稣说的无所不在，胜过

汽车、电脑、导弹，胜过宇宙飞船
胜过一万年所有的科学的钢铁花朵
和显微镜下人造干细胞的精密技术

n. 让爱行动起来

街道没任何征兆就下塌了一块
城市不知不觉中沉降了几厘米
墙体开裂如狰狞无声的哭，地震的

影子隐隐巨大。强拆问题，三鹿奶粉
问题，都是他娘的钱闹的，急得
我差点学狗叫，学那忠实的动物

让爱行动起来，学做面部松弛操
我的同胞们，别表情严肃刀枪不入
尽管我的反复强调，经常受同事讥笑

把爱接通到人心里去，以免缺血
紊乱、梗死。接通到企业、机关里去
单位也许就开始有点人的样子

有爱的人是从内向外的美，尽管遭到
权力和金钱诋毁。政府如果无法让爱像
货币一样流通，它就该天天给自己放假

解散突发事件办公室，减少税负
减少警察和城管、环境污染之虞，让
薪水坐上行电梯，物价坐下行电梯

15. 中华民族到了最危险的时候

——（中）田汉

O. 高悬之剑

一百年来最伟大的汉语诗句
"最危险的时候"，一个民族
对准了一首诗歌的腰部

最危险的时候，不在 1911 年
不在 1937、1946、1989 年
在今天，就在我们面前

就在于信仰倒地，道德狼藉
即使天才创造出崭新的文体
所有锦绣文章也只能是病句

o. 我的祈愿

假如一个民族优秀的大脑接踵病变
蛛网萦结，堕落倾圮，谎言恣肆
一个民族就到了最危险的时候

假如商人愈加贪婪无忌且愚蠢
试图在每张钞票上写下自己的名字
一个民族就到了最危险的时候

假如人民以自己是人民感到耻辱
蚂蚁在树洞里不再思想劳动
一个民族就到了最危险的时候

假如河流被污浊裹挟，发出蒙克的
呼喊，清凉的风视而不见；假如
众多的基因被改写，生命在

萌芽中便丧失了活力，一个民族
就到了最危险的时候。语言成了喘息
韵脚成了垃圾，翻滚着，弥漫着

先生，你早就看到了这些？
才悲愤地写下刺骨锥痛的诗句？
先生，我们怎么做，你才肯安息？

16. 在今天的时代，诗人何为？

—— （德）海德格尔

P. 写诗与诗歌史

诗人何为？当然要写诗。把诗
写在"A4"纸上，写在大腿上
跟着那大腿大大咧咧走进诗歌史

一路上赶着追着那美腿，猛跑
从隐喻，到拒绝隐喻，到
下半身，多加进叙事成分

把叙事叙到琐碎、琐碎不堪
把文化写到与文化无关的程度
把诗歌史写到遗忘了诗歌的程度

p. 在视觉时代也听听声音

暂闭上眼，回忆发潮的磁带
带划痕的旧唱片。坎坎伐檀的
音韵因为森林保护法而成绝响

石磨给驴子的蹄音轻打着节拍
我们想挽留古人只拽住了
他的衣裳，衣袖断裂云飞扬

当年野合的恋人正喊着开房
听收割机的响动，吃撑了农药的
麦苗噌噌地长，通向城市的道路

加油站收费站林立，歌星的体型
膨胀，大过整个广场的假唱
楼角转出整容后的邻居女郎

听听小学的读书声，中学的已经
不需要听，听听教育体制的绝望
捂住耳朵钻进草垛也能听见呼救

多来米法索拉西，印钞机拉稀
银行窃喜。一二三四五六七
数字发声之后变成物质之欲

17. 你选择什么样的存在，完全取决于自己

—— （法）萨特

Q. 我和萨特也许有一面之缘

七年前在巴黎，曾多次经过
他经常光顾的小酒馆，想象
他抽着烟斗，小酌在临窗的桌前

今日我走在北京的街道，望着
匆忙的黄皮肤的脸庞，和我认识
的人招呼，与不熟识的人微笑

我就得到一个近乎美好的下午
就像是劳有所获，又像是意外之财
又像与萨特一起数着自己的脚步

q. 某一天和我自己

中午拒绝了一位巧舌如簧的
保健品推销员上门服务
下午"忘记"了一次"重要"会议

读 50 分钟《史记》、半小时
英语新闻，写书法九幅——
其中模仿郑燮的那张最为精到

看楼下的草地茵茵，看窗外的
小雨打湿天气预报的阴转多云
夜间有梦，因几只蚊子引起

蚊香是伪劣产品。起身写一篇
《"盘峰论剑"只是我早餐和午餐
之间的一次自我矛盾》的文章

"煤球是黑的"和"元宵是白的"
都对，但都自说自话，却没提
它们都是圆的。接着复又睡下

明天早起跑步，之后到学校授课
把学生教成油盐不进的饱学之士
或不小心以误人子弟为己任

18. 断竹，续竹，飞土，逐肉

——（中）《上古歌谣·弹歌》

R. 观看古人狩猎

我们看到，一位先民劈砍竹子，嚓嚓
制作一张弓，嘣嘣；把石块嘭地弹出
一只鸟应声倒地，一堆篝火燃起

我们想象他健劲的肌肉，赤足行走如飞
黑红的脸膛，粗布围腰，像一幅画
连续播放，被识文断字的人写进诗行

而写诗者并不曾称自己很有诗才
行为艺术和文字，都为我们青睐
虽说一个性感精彩，一个略显苍白

r. 女孩君娜

一个山东日照的女孩君娜
一个黑发飘柔顾盼生情的女孩
君娜，宁静平和的她

一个曾不停周旋在男孩子中间
以博得频频约会而自得的君娜
一个稍翻翻书就轻易得"A"的

君娜，如今孜孜为母尽孝，对妹妹
呵护有加。一个从南加州学成了
电影专业回国的——她，发誓为

认识和不认识的人做一千件善事
再做一千件。要用自己的虔诚之心
证明所有人都是弥足珍贵的

"呵呵，应该的，举手之劳啊！"
有这"举手之劳"，世界就不同以往
我不再疑惑于诗，于美丽

太太碰碰我，说你是不是爱上她了？
我想了想，答"是"。我们抬头
夏夜的星星渺远，满含爱和悲哀

19. 这世界就是舞台，可角色分配得不像样子

—— （英）王尔德

S. 伟大，或那耳熟能详的角色

大官并不伟大，大款并不伟大
艺术大师记不清自己家在哪
当今的伟大人物，就像被孩子

用草帽扣住的那只蚂蚱。奥巴马
算不上英明，阿萨德也不行
狼眼睛的普京只是个爱掰手腕的总统

伟大只是穿行于人间的风，朴素而
敏感的心灵，绝望伸出的树叶般众多的
手，拽紧发疯的机车，到最后一分钟

s. 做回自己

不知还能否随时打开好奇心的卷帘
我的想象，常常比暴雨前燕子
灰白的腹部还低，还忧郁

我在纸上写下：做自己，做回自己
这浅浅的字迹我至今是否已涂改？
做自己，我能做到哪里？

戴上圣哲智慧脑回下的清澈目光？
重新长出年轻时浑圆的肱二头肌？
保持与生俱来的善良木讷？也许

换种活法更适合我的才能和天性？
中学老师点名，我响亮地答"到"
如今冷淡了很多人，他爱谁谁去

只有见到孩子们我才深弯下腰
已老花的眼眸看到"母亲"这个词
依旧会噙满泪水。此刻的我

不过是我大半生光阴的一个碎片
我满把的诗像十根手指不一般齐
它们概莫能外——终将零落成泥

20. 我们只能享有我们所能理解的幸福

—— （比）梅特林克

T. 彼时异地

我曾在圣地亚哥海滩流连
第七舰队的航母静静在旁边
它没开炮我已经中弹；我曾经

在凯旋门通达的街衢徜徉
商店里挤满抢购 LV 包的中国人
和间或羡慕间或鄙夷的目光

在汉语被称作"华语"的狮城
喷水池一侧；在暹罗湾夜市
被灯红酒绿捉摸，引逗挑唆

t. 诗与时代：下行音阶

偶遇一首诗，偶遇一种心情
在湖州南浔古镇，在小莲庄
梦里也在其它许多地方

抬头有气势非凡的牌匾
我一步迈进月亮里去
不是月亮，是月亮门

门内是什么摇弋着季节？
——好一派西湖景色
不是西湖，是这庄园中荷塘

举起西湖一样的绿伞、花朵
的粉红娇艳和杨万里的诗篇
我好似周朝的采诗官，吟唱

"荷叶田田"。我不是采诗官
是个游客，来此只为和门票相关
迎面有这家主人刘镛带来的一阵风

不是刘镛，是面容姣好的讲解员
一位女性，在谈论风。不是风
是当年刘镛抱拳迎客的豪爽风度

21. 吾日三省吾身

——（中）曾子

U. 在纷纭的斜体字中间

风是斜的，雨是斜的，倨傲的手
斜插在兜里。错币上面领袖的表情
不端正。斜的还包括明星大佬们

龙飞凤舞的签名。追光的谄媚中
T型台上模特们双脚交叉走猫步
迎来爆炒腰花般的掌声。让人纠结啊

甚至那一抹夕阳，都不肯垂直落下去
我提气，深呼吸，每日三省乎己
在饭前饭后之间的半小时内

u. 记下我们对语言所犯的罪行

就像一个人自首，对自己从良的后果
有些害怕。身边，生存仍旧在
苟且这台购物机上奋勇地刷卡；希望

是小溪豢养的鱼，数不清的尖嘴鹤
围聚在这里；诗歌的手臂已经脱臼
她扶不起那个叫做现实的大脑袋

人民被催肥，肚腹里装满困顿、焦躁
肠胀气、前列腺炎，等等。但人民
还没胖到不会游泳也沉不下去的程度

时间被兑换成零钱，兑换成钢镚的脸
钢镚和钢镚拥挤在一起，你埋怨我
我仇恨你，嗫嚅的一生不如个响屁

唯有自尊，说出来我就自责就想哭
唯有自尊像一块还不太脏的粗布
我们用它做成旗子还是做成短裤？

我们对语言犯下的罪不能轻饶
连先民们都知道，遮羞很重要
大伙不能裸着身子跟着旗子跑

22. 荣誉就像玩具，只能玩玩而已

—— （波）居里夫人

V. 孩童演绎着成人世界

我五岁的儿子在堆积木，旁边放着
他昨天的手工，和几朵小红花
他神态专注，拼起一座房子

一边和自己说：陆圣得搭得最好
然后把一朵花自缀胸前，得意非凡
其实他昨天的房子比今天盖的漂亮

今天没有好房子，但必须有奖励
我们成人何尝不如此，自己定规矩
自己表彰自己。煞有介事，乐此不疲

v. 规则与标准

成人的可笑之处不仅于此
用自身的尺度衡量所有身外之物
比如大象大，以我们个头作比较

比如用自己的大腿，和别人的
手指比；用释迦牟尼和约翰比
打擂双方不用比赛，谁长着黑头发

谁胜利。或者只懂一个英语单词
"Yes"。所谓朋友、敌人
就是切身利益的同谋或对立面

我看见，三分之一的国家元首
患有道德顽症；道德家的面目
十分可疑。人类像疯长的野草

没有给地球带来多少价值意义
一群人的荣耀，是另一群人的
毒药，唯有平淡平安或可期许

我的名字是一个简单的符号
几捺几撇，我的额头想大写人生
却被我萎琐的尾巴拖进小写

23. 我的志愿就是作一个小诗人，而我早已到达

——（阿根廷）博尔赫斯

W. 博尔赫斯尚且如此

我们所有的诗人都是小人物
我们的我们加起来成为一个
残缺不全的大诗人。博尔赫斯

已从容抵达，我们还在路上
在欲望沉浮中听从时光的指令
享受指甲盖大小的幸福生涯

是一粒黑痣一般的光荣
是一次癌变一样的光荣
是我们从来没有获得过的光荣

w. 我曾想，但没做到，我仍在想

我曾想，做一个赫赫有名的诗人
像海涅那样，"说出了天下最好的
名姓，也就说出了我的姓名"

我曾想，诗歌已经包罗万象
已不需要再续貂劳神，可我
听见心里的一个声音说不

我曾想，写一千首好诗
以一千个化名投递出去
而发表了诗歌的报刊寄来

又被退回，原因只在——
"查无此人"；我一边做工
一边漫游天下，像惠特曼那样

不放过每个角落、每一份细小的
善良和美。我一笔一划耐心描绘
轻轻地吟诵不惊动一丝虫鸣

我一边写一边感慨，这些细微的
美丽才是普通人的上乘之作
这世上只有诗篇，没有诗人

24. 采菊东篱下，悠然见南山

—— （中）陶渊明

X. 菊及其根系

菊花的根系是东方魅力的面目
我凭借芬芳一缕回到唐，回到
晋朝的消息。菊，卓然而花瓣纷披

馨香播远，尤胜过妖艳世俗的牡丹
菊，自矜之花，君子之尊，即使风中
相互触碰，也只传递信息和友善

我要用文学史的完整一章来谈陶潜
在王府井大街背诵桃花源
让天底下的人物植物都听见

x. 自然中的水泥森林

朋友搬家到郊外去了，去作一朵
清淡的白云。谁的梦里没有一片
晴朗的天，不想让皱纹舒展

朋友是古典美学教授，新居是
俄式典雅小楼，湘南民居式内装修
我戏称笔挺的西服里衬着肚兜

多少房间？陶渊明预言过的——
"八九间"。客厅监控镜头对着
发财树，哪有什么"鸡鸣桑树巅"

庭院种满茄子辣椒一应绿色蔬菜
草坪铲掉，"豆苗"自给，半月十天
不出门，"悠然"住在水泥森林里

我送的《高山隐士图》往哪儿挂？
拿回去，我嘈杂的内心也挂不下
既然原谅了自己，就只能原谅他

就像我只是在写诗时，才记起
仁义礼智的原有之意。我一次次
失信于自己，带上脸谱才出门去

25. 你再没有可能被绊倒，在你自行选择的小径上

—— （古埃及）《亡灵书》

Y. 科学是试错，人生也是

我曾仆身跌倒，被某种念头推拒
一股冲动，两缕情绪，三个词
没说出的话，半拉貌似新鲜的比喻

使我流血。那次无辜的行径像罪恶
语句的模棱两可——差点卖了本人
意象的陷阱，和摇摇欲坠的篇章结构

所谓艺术的创造、思潮、理念
我都向同伴借过，包括荣誉的迷魂香
于今冷汗涔涔，当时自以为得计

y. 众人的路，自己的路

年轻时奔跑的兔子，并没有讥讽我
如今的龟步。我步履已迟缓
诗行中用着越来越多的标点

下体无力，晨勃日见其少。这事
我不愿提起，它是我的秘密。我的
生活，说挣扎说奋斗均无不可

我借着白发在夜里读书，镜片
和偶发的灵感疾病一样闪烁
傍晚我刚刚完成 40 分钟锻炼

30 年来，一天天朝着自己的目标
砥砺行走，我调整那目标，方向
我踩出的小路已逐渐离开别人

我所有的仇恨都已经丢弃
妒能之心像荒年的米缸已经见底
它们一次次重来，一次次减弱

要洗涮掉自己的污浊真不容易
行走的人不会忘了亲爱的兄弟
我祝福他们，也没忘了自己

26. 天黑前路途遥遥，天黑前路途遥遥

—— （美）弗罗斯特

Z. 像弗罗斯特那样感知，感动，感恩

作为乡间医生的弗罗斯特
仔细丈量脚下道路的弗罗斯特
你摸到了生存的命脉，所以说出

你回到事物的根，接近真理
我仿佛伴随你，行走在田埂
引颈仰望星空的无比辽阔

为卑微的人们和自己写下诗章
轻声颂祷，麦花香和上天的垂顾
日复一日，在时间的肋骨穿过

z. 夜间的颂祷

而此刻，喧嚣的声音逐渐消弭
安静如夜间开放之花蕾，我耳边
有个声音说正是写诗的时候

有个声音说正是颂祷的时候
我已经放弃了全知的视角
自己做主把日常生活的节奏还原

还原为一种慢，与文字携手
穿越在城乡呼喊不回头的春天
于人世间活成一堆废铜烂铁

或一块湿润的泥土，面向但丁
则只是一种彻头彻尾的绝望
我们，一群美轮美奂的小诗人

一群被称诗人就只好羞愧的工匠
面对穹苍，俯察凡尘的面相
记录这岌岌可危的世界

与微不足道的诗句交换手稿
此刻，我心潮涌起，黯然神伤
泪水在我脸上凝结着秋天的微凉

2012 年 1—9 月，北京

评论篇

陆健诗歌的心路历程

单占生

自上世纪八十年代以降，中国新诗坛出现过许多思潮，也出现过自认或公认的流派诗歌群体，如"朦胧派诗群""新现实主义诗群""他们诗群""非非主义诗群""莽汉主义诗群""园明圆诗群""神性写作诗群""新乡土诗派诗群""知识分子写作诗群""民间写作诗群""第三条道路写作诗群""下半身诗群"以及"中间代诗群"再及许许多多具有地方特色的诗群。如果我们仅从这些诗群中寻找陆健的名字是很难找到的。但陆健、陆健的诗以及陆健诗的影响自上世纪八十年代以降都是实实在在存在着。在一次"陆健诗歌创作研讨会"上，诗人叶延滨指出，"陆健的诗歌是非常值得研究的一个现象，因为陆健在当代诗歌中是一个比较独特的诗人，他的诗歌创作30年，在诸多的风潮、流派中保持了自己的创作的个性……在各个风潮中不同的领军人物逐渐消失的时候，陆健仍然占据着他自己的位置。"叶延滨的这段话说于2007年5月10日上午，时间已经又流逝了五年，叶延滨对陆健的评价依然准确、深刻。而陆健五年之后呈献给诗坛的新诗集《一位美轮美奂的小诗人之歌》，则更进一步强化了叶延滨这段话的价值与意义。

其实，在过去的几十年里，对陆健诗歌的研究一直没有间断过。据我所知，最早的评价文章是刘士林写的对陆健诗歌的欣赏性文章，接下来是由我写的对陆健早期诗作的综合评价文字，文章的题目是《人的力量，心的灵视》。陆健的名作《名城与门》出版后，著名诗歌评论家沈奇写过一篇对陆健来说特别有价值的文章，题目叫作《诗城独门》，这是对陆健诗集《名城与门》的评价，也是对陆健诗歌创作的评价。另一位法门独到的诗评家杨吉哲对陆健的长诗创作有过一篇题目为《论陆健的长诗创作》的长文，对陆健创作的"以外国历史人物、事件为题材"的长诗系列《日内瓦的太阳》进行了综合研究，认为陆健不仅"把我们拖向了时间深处，拖向物质力量和生命意识的角斗场中，让我们看到一幕前所未有的戏剧"，同时这些长诗也呈现出作者"杰出的陈述"能力。此后，在陆健的四本纪实性诗作出版之后，中国传媒大学于 2007 年召开过一次陆健诗歌创作研讨会，会议发布了一个研讨会纪要（见 2007 年 5 月《文艺报》），认为"他是一个值得研究的'诗歌现象'"。会上，屠岸、叶延滨、李小雨、唐晓渡、周月亮、王燕生、林莽、张清华、朱先树、何晓兵、徐刚等诸位诗人、评论家、教授都对陆健的诗表达了自己独到的看法，认为陆健是一位"不可复制的诗人"。据我所知，对陆健诗创作的评价文章远不止这些（其中部分文章见诸篇幅达 172000 字的陆健诗歌研究专著，1997 年 2 月版百花文艺出版社《关于一个诗人》一书）。我在这里转述不同时期的评论家对陆健诗的评价，只是想借此提出一个问题：作为一种"现象"存在的陆健，到底是怎样的一种"现象"呢？

　　"诗城独门""不可复制的诗人""一个值得研究的诗歌现象"，这样的评论分别出自诗人、诗歌评论家沈奇、匡满和叶延滨先生之口，亦应是诸多诗人和评论家对陆健的共有认识。那么，陆健能够成为三十年来中国诗坛的一种特殊"现象"，又具有怎样的一种特殊性和可资研究的价值与意义呢？这里，我想借用一下李犁在其论文《救诗与救世：陆健诗歌的写作动机和价值》（见 2012 年 7 月版《诗林》杂志）的一句话来表达我的认识。他说："陆健诗歌写作的最大贡献就是在原来诗歌美学范畴之外给我们提供了一种新的写作可能。"李犁的这句话所针对的是陆健从 2003 年开始写的四本纪实性诗歌。其实，如果我们大体回顾一下陆健的诗歌创作历程，就会发现，陆健始终是站在他创作的那个诗坛的当下审美范畴的流行话语之外进行他的诗歌创作的。站在风潮之外，探寻诗歌审美的新的可能，始终伴随着陆健诗歌创作的主体意识和实践行为。如果我们采取简单化的方式把陆健三十年来的诗切成四段，我们就会更为清晰地看清陆健诗歌创作的心路历程和审美变异踪迹，亦可更为切实地认识陆健诗歌创作的特性和其价值意义。

陆健的诗歌创作起始于上世纪八十年代初，当时诗坛的主要思潮是"朦胧诗"的"诗潮"，当时亦称"新思潮"。应该说，处于当时诗坛的诗人，莫不受到朦胧诗的影响与冲击。陆健受此影响也是显在的。与不少诗人随着朦胧诗的思潮而进行创作不同，陆健在受朦胧诗影响的同时，又在朦胧诗思潮的基础上向前迈出了新的步伐。朦胧诗对当时诗坛的影响可以从两个方面来考察。其一，对社会和人的认识观念上的影响。其二，对诗歌艺术手段和形式方面的影响。在对社会观念的影响方面，其主要成就是对"文革"及"文革"后的极左思潮进行了严厉的政治批判。在对人的认识的影响方面，其主要成是朦胧诗通过诗作和诗歌理论的阐释强力张扬了大写的"人"，彰显了人的尊严。在艺术影响方面，朦胧诗以其略带现代艺术特征的艺术样态，对新中国成立后三十年的诗歌艺术进行了彻底的颠覆。应该说，朦胧诗对中国诗坛的影响是深广持久的。而在朦胧诗思潮的巨大影响下走上诗坛的陆健，却在朦胧诗的影响下向人性的深度和艺术的前沿进行了新的探索。如果说朦胧诗在社会问题与人性问题上的彰显上强化了人性的丰富性的话，那么，陆健则在其诗中彰显了社会与人生的复杂性。不用翻看陆健当时的诗集，我很清晰地记得陆健当时的一首短诗叫作《美丽天真善良与悲剧》。诗中写到花的美丽，蝴蝶的美丽，花的自在，蝴蝶的自由。当花与蝴蝶都各自独立存在之时，他们的美，他们的自在与自由都是真实存在的。但悲剧的发生则恰恰就在两种美的"亲近"。当蝴蝶扑向美丽的花朵的怀抱之时，当美丽的花朵以自己美丽的热情拥抱美丽的蝴蝶之时，花的毒粉却导致了蝴蝶的死亡，蝴蝶的气息也导致了花朵的枯萎。在探索人性与社会的复杂性的同时，在诗歌艺术上，陆健一改朦胧诗的感伤与缠绵，也一改朦胧诗常用的介于象征与比喻之间的修辞手段为对表现对象直接书写，并把这直接的书写在整首诗作的框架内转换为隐喻，使自己的诗呈现出一种具有先锋性的硬朗风格。此时陆健的诗似有一层坚硬的外壳，但这硬壳内有着陆健对社会人生的理性思考。从某种意义上讲，陆健从一开始就是把自己的诗歌创作定位在"智性"创作这一基点之上的。也许正是有了这个前提，他的诗才和他的这个人一样，总给人一种棱角分明的硬汉感受。时间悄无声息地流逝，许多事情转瞬即成过去。在我们回过头来再去察看那过去的事物时，似乎总会发现许多不言自明的地方。比如我们站在今天去考察陆健当时的诗风，就会很自然地发现，陆健此后诗歌题材与写作风格的变异与坚守，恰为当时陆健尽快摆脱朦胧诗的影响而追寻自己的诗歌立场独立作了注脚。

自陆健对朦胧诗影响的成功摆脱以降，至今日他写出《一位美轮美奂的小诗人之歌》，这中间，陆健的诗曾有过两次对自己前期诗歌创作风格的摆脱与超越。近几十年中国诗坛的现实证明，一个有才华的诗人，摆脱与超越当下诗潮的影响并不是一件难以做到的事情，但摆脱与超越自己已有的风格并能坚守自己的诗歌观念与立场的确很难，但陆健做到了。我想，这也许正是叶延滨认为陆健是一个值得研究的诗歌现象的原因所在。而更为重要的是，陆健在摆脱与超越自己的同时，两次创造性变异都为自己写出《一位美轮美奂的小诗人之歌》打下了坚实的基础。当我们回过头来把陆健的诗歌创作历程放在中国诗坛近三十年的行进历程中进行比对研究之时，就更能认清陆健按照自己的诗歌立场和观念进行属于自己的创造劳动的重要与可贵。对中国近三十年的诗人来说，有一种魔咒似乎很难逃脱。这个魔咒就是诗坛一而再再而三的对前代诗人的颠覆性写作。一次次的颠覆完成了对中国诗坛的极左化意识形态写作的格局，同时也忽略了中国诗坛自新诗开创以来的文化传统和诗性意识，进而使颠覆变成了只是为了完成颠覆这一事实或事件的使命。而陆健从进入诗坛之始，就没有把颠覆性写作注入自己的思域。他站在历次诗潮与流派之外，富有激情地进行着属于他自己的创作。其实，我无意在这里对颠覆性写作进行批评。从某种意义上讲，对于颠覆性写作我还是要给以充分肯定的。但是，我还想指出的一个事实是中国新诗自一开始就担负着颠覆与建构的双重使命。在新诗草创时期，不少人认为新诗只是破坏一种旧形式，创建一个新的形式。而自象征派诗在中国新诗坛传播之后，大家才逐步认识到，对于中国的新诗坛而言，要颠覆或者叫作"革命"的不仅仅是一种旧的诗体形式，更重要的是还有对自己的心智进行革命性颠覆。因之，"革命"与"颠覆"自然也就成了一种中国新诗发展的潜在和显在的动力。无论是"向西走"还是"向东走"，这种动力会如影随形地伴随在诗人左右。自上世纪八十年代以降，以颠覆为写作动力不仅成了诗坛的一种常见现象，甚或可以认为不少诗人把这种"颠覆"性写作视作一种"诗道"，也是可以通过"颠覆"使自己迅疾成名的"王道"。这样一来，在中国新诗坛原初本具有诗性意义的"革命"与"颠覆"就在一次次的"王道"实践中被"异化"得一派狼藉。实话说，对于一个长期浸淫在诗坛情境中的人来说，面对如此现实，无论采取怎样的一种方式来保持自己的独立与自足，都不是一件易事。

陆健真正走上独立自足的艺术自觉，是从上个世纪 90 年代初开始，能证明他诗歌创作独立自足意识清醒自觉的标志，是《名城与门》和《日内瓦的太阳》两部诗集的出版。《名城与门》（1992 年 9 月文化艺术出版社版）这部诗集由六十六首既独立又相互关联的诗作组成了一个宏阔的历史空间，而构成这个宏大历史时空的诗性元素，则是诗人陆健对中国现当代四十八位文化名人与艺术大师的叙写，也是诗人与四十八位中国现当代文化心灵的对话。更应引起我们注意的是，这四十八位中国现当代文化名人或者叫作四十八尊文化心灵，被诗人陆健分别安放在十三首同名为《门》的诗为间隔的诗性空间之内，这样，这部诗集就构成了一个巨大的城邦时空，同时也构成了诗人宏阔的心灵时空。与《名城与门》同时出版的陆健的另一部诗集《日内瓦的太阳》（1992年10月台湾诗之华出版社版），则由书写西方历史文化名人的七部长诗构成。这其中所涉及的人物，有伊丽莎白二世、阿基米德、亚历山大、爱因斯坦、劳伦斯与弗里达、凡高、加尔文等人。对这两部诗集，著名评论家沈奇和杨吉哲分别有过非常有见地的评价。沈奇在其评价陆健的诗集《名城与门》的长篇论文中，称陆健的诗为"诗城独门"，说陆健"为我们开启了一扇特异不凡的独在之门"。沈奇不仅从诗的题材的特殊性所展示的历史空间、结构的特殊性所呈现的交响乐式的史诗气势、语言的特殊性所产生的诗性张力，更为重要的是，沈奇在其文章开头所提出的陆健在当时的诗坛的特殊性的问题。尽管沈奇在当时对此问题没有作更为深入的论述，但今天看来，沈奇在当时就能论及这一问题，更能让人臣服沈奇眼光的独到和对诗坛认识的深刻。在沈奇看来，在一次次的诗潮尘埃落定，当我们"反思、梳理与整合"诗坛的历史经验之时，我们就不应该再次"忽略"那些曾被我们"一再疏忽了"的那些"冷静而沉着地游离于"潮流之外，"对整个现代主义新诗潮做深层参与且保持独立诗性和超越目光的，可称为边缘性诗人的从作品到人格的关注和研究"。距沈奇说出这样观念，时间已走过十六个年头。现在，我们用沈奇的观念再去观照陆健，我们更能看出沈奇当时的清醒与深刻，亦更能看出陆健在当时之于诗坛的价值。

　　需要特别指出的是，我们今天说的问题，不仅仅是沈奇以上的论断和认识，我们是想从陆健《名城与门》以及《日内瓦的太阳》两本诗集来考察陆健心灵时空的开拓向度问题。从实际的情况看，陆健创作自始至今的独立诗性精神和人格品质已是大家的一个共识。我们今天之所以探讨陆健诗歌的心灵空间的向度与变异历程，其目的是想从这个角度以陆健为一个个案提出中国新诗人的心灵格局的问题。我个人认为，在我们历经了长时期的追求自我呈现诗歌创作之后，这个问题的提出对中国诗坛的长远发展会有一定的参考价值。与此同时，我们也可以通过对这两本诗集所呈现出的诗人陆健心灵空间的考察，更为清楚地认清陆健前后几本诗作为什么做出此样的选择而非彼样的选择的内在联系。

如前所述，陆健在其《名城与门》中以立体式的形式建构构筑了一座中国现当代文化的心灵城堡，而在《日内瓦的太阳》中，陆健则通过对西方圣哲的诗性陈述，给我们构筑了一片人类共有的精神天空并对这一澄明中隐含着晦暗的天空进行了深度反思。需要指出的一点是，陆健在对西方圣哲的思想行为进行反思时，不仅持据深远、厚重的东方文化立场，同时把西方圣哲的思想行为，放在人类思想行为的一种超越种族和地域的形而上的层面上进行咀嚼。在如此的反思中，既有人类生活的经验性思考，也有一种超越性目光。对于《日内瓦的太阳》这部诗集的几首长诗，评论家杨吉哲有过独到且深刻的评价。他说："陆健对人类生活的许多方面进行了思索追问，战争、和平、宗教、性爱、艺术及流行的社会病症，等等，都在他的文字中呈现与展开，并趋向凝重与透彻，其中包蕴了人类漫长的身体力行和苦思求索所达到的智慧高度。"（杨吉哲《论陆健的长诗创作》）就《名城与门》与《日内瓦的太阳》而言，沈奇与杨吉哲对其进行的解读与评价是目光独到，慧心独运的。这里，我之所以反复再三推介沈奇与吉哲对陆健诗的评价，是因为他们二位的确认识到陆健诗中不同寻常的诗性元素。这种不同寻常的诗性元素即陆健诗中呈现给我们的超越时代的诗性时空。我们应该切实看出，陆健此时思维时空的远足，是那个时代中国诗坛所独有的现象。陆健此时的心灵远足，不仅奠定了他自己独立自足的诗性观念，同时也为当时的国内诗坛注入了一种新的风气，使当时中国诗坛的心灵时空得以更大范围的拓展。此后的陆健，也因了此次远足得以进入没有羁绊的创造之境。

如果说陆健的《名城与门》《日内瓦的太阳》完成了他的一次关于诗的天空远足理想的话，那么，标志着陆健的创作进入了另一个全新阶段的诗集则是《温暖》（2008年12月辽宁人民出版社）的出版。《温暖》集结了陆健自2004至2007年创作的四本诗集，分别为《34份礼物》《田楼，田楼》《枫叶上的比尔》《洛水之阳》。四本诗集呈现了陆健生命历程中的点滴刻痕。《洛水之阳》写他故乡和故乡的亲朋，这是他生命底色和性灵的根脉；《枫叶上的比尔》写他的儿子，也是他的家庭；《田楼，田楼》是他离开故乡走向社会，走近泥土的驿站；而《34份礼物》是他与他的学生的对话，其实也隐喻着他与社会的交互关系。故乡、家庭、社会，家人、邻居、同学、乡亲、老师、亲朋、父母、学生，他与这些人或者说这些人与他的关联，彰显出他生活的质感，也昭示出他生命的体验。其实，应进一步指出的并不仅是这些，不是他写了什么以及怎么写的，而是他从《名城与门》《日内瓦的太阳》的历史时空走进现实时空这一变化，以及这种变化对他的创作来说所昭示的意义与价值。从诗性心灵的远游到切实感受自己身边的人和事，从飞扬的想象联想到白描式的陈述，陆健完成了一个从天空到大地的转换，这使得他的诗获得具有无限张力的历史纵深。由宏阔的历史时空到具体、细部的现实时空，由高处在天空的圣哲先贤到生长在泥土里的诗人身边生活着生存着的普通人，从放浪的想象到原生态的直写，使得他的诗思和诗艺都得以全方位的拓展，也为他后来的创作奠定了坚实根基。从此，他的创作获得了充分的自由。

从这里开始，让我们进入对《一位美轮美奂的小诗人之歌》的解读。从某种意义上来说，在此之前我们对于陆健诗的分段描述，似乎并不仅仅是为了解读那个阶段的陆健，而更有从那个时期那个地点出发走向这里走向此时的意味。这让我想起佛教修行的"四道"。按照中华佛教百科全书对"四道"的解释，佛教修行所指的"四道"，是指断烦恼、证真理、得涅槃的四个阶段，即加行道、无间道、解脱道、胜进道。"加行道"又作方便道，是为断除烦恼所做的预备性修行；"无间道"又作无碍道，是修行者直接断除烦恼的阶段；"解脱道"是于无间道之后生起一念正智证悟真理，为悟得真理、解脱烦恼的阶段；"胜进道"又名胜道，是指解脱之后增进定慧的时期。笔者无意把佛教修行的"四道"与陆健创作的几个阶段作生硬的比附，只是觉得佛教修行四道的过程与陆健的诗歌创作有诸多相似之处。王国维在《人间词话》中也有做人为诗的"三境界"之说。在他看来，人生想成就大事业者必经三种境界：第一境，昨夜西风凋碧树，独上高楼，望断天涯路；第二境，衣带渐宽终不悔，为伊消得人憔悴；第三境，众里寻得千百度，蓦然回首，那人却在灯火阑珊处。王国维是在说人生，但因是用诗来说，后人也就以此为诗人作诗的三大境界认之。其实，做人作诗都是一样的。成就任何事情似应都要经历一个过程。走到最后，都是要看结果如何。求得正果，证得真理，看到"那人"，才可见出这过程中所蕴含的超乎寻常的意义与价值，才可真正见出这过程中每个链条的不可或缺，才可见这链条的最近一个环节所携带的心灵时空之间的关联。我们平时所说的事后诸葛亮，也许就是这个道理。这里我们也以一个事后诸葛亮的身份，再去观照一下《一位美轮美奂的小诗人之歌》，我们亦可发现，陆健此时的创作已达无间无碍的自由创造之境，而他的作品，同时携带了他前此创作诗性心灵时空的所有信息。如果让我们换一种思维方式来看待这一问题，我们亦可见出，陆健当下的诗正是有了前此的深广积淀，才有可能进入今天自由境界的创作。

那么，《一位美轮美奂的小诗人之歌》又呈现给我们一些什么值得思考的东西呢？笔者认为，以下几点似乎应该引起我们的关注。

其一，诗歌形式建构的仪式性存在。

《一位美轮美奂的小诗人之歌》是一部诗集，又是一部前后圆合建构匠心独具的组诗。也许正是这样一部诗集，强化了我对陆健诗歌创作在形式建构上的仪式性行为的关注。《一位美轮美奂的小诗人之歌》共计 26 首，严格讲是 26 组。每组诗由一个总题引领，用阿拉伯数字标序；在大的题目之下，有先后两个小的题目，用英文字母标序，前者为大写，后者为小写。前者 3 段，后者 6 段，每段皆为 3 行。例如第一首："1 我对自己说吉约姆是你来的时候了——（法）吉约姆·阿波利奈"，这是大题；下面一组诗的题目为："A 阿波利奈能来我当然也能""a '我'的含义"。26 组诗从 A、a 到 Z、z，构成了 26 个英文字母的首尾整合，也构成了一个可以进行无限自由创造独立自足的空间。一组诗是一个小的独立自足的诗性空间，一部诗是一个大的独立自足的诗性空间。这样的组合在形式建构上有着严格的规律，而在内容的选择上则有着无限的自由。把严格的规律与充分的自由结合在一起，其实是陆健诗歌创作长期坚持的基本现实，也是中国诗歌乃至世界诗歌长期呈现给我们的基本规律。由此，我们可以想起陆健的《名城与门》，想起中国的古典诗歌，想起西方的十四行诗，更让我们想起诗的仪式性存在这个问题。

毋庸置疑，在涉及文学的所有文体中，诗的文体是一种极其特殊的形式。这种文体特殊就特殊在它不仅仅是一种文字呈现样态，而且还是一种仪式性存在，是一个有着仪式性介质的场。在这个具有仪式性的场域，文字所指涉的现实事物或者在此发生了变异，或者在某些方面得以强化或弱化。当一个诗人连同他的写作对象进入这个仪式性场中时，他不再是一个生活在世俗世界的凡人，而是一个沉浸在诗性仪式并具有诗性思维的诗人。写作在此时此地成为一种仪式性行为。诗人通过仪式性行为超脱出现实世界进入另一个空间当中成就个人的反思与冥想，完成自己的诗性经验。这里需要特别说明的一点是，诗的此种仪式性存在在中国古典诗体形式上呈现得比较明显，而新诗则很难使诗仪式性存在通过形式感得以呈现。因为藉由仪式所进入的空间既然是一个神圣的空间，这中间当然就有许多规范，而这些规范也会反复显现在诗歌形式之中，并成为一个作品内在的、合乎逻辑的推动力量，也成为诗人创作行为和诗歌作品成形的图腾标识。中国的古典诗歌、西方的十四行诗都充分利用了仪式性的形态动力和标识暗示，新诗则把这一诗性动力及标识弱化了。对于更加趋向于"思"与"批判"的新诗而言，失去这一仪式性的形态动力，应该是一件自然而然的事。因为"思"的自由弥散也许并不必须借助某件规范或者说"思"的自由弥散本身就不适宜有过多的规范。但是，如果我们站有"诗"的立场而不仅仅是"思"的立场上来思考这一问题，我们把"思"放在"诗"的场中来思考这一问题，也许就会发现诗的仪式性存在对于诗的非凡性、神圣性是多么的重要。把"思"放在"仪式"性的形态之中，让"思"不失其自由与敏锐，使诗呈现出具有仪式性图腾感的形式存在，这大概应是一个有价值的想法。如能在此方面做一些探索，那就是一种有价值的诗性行为。有意思的是陆健不仅这样做了，而且做得很有意味。也许，陆健并没有如笔者说的这样去想，但他作的诗的仪式性形式探索，的确给了我们许多启发，同时也使他的诗作更具诗性。他为他自己和他的写作对象构筑一个"场"，这个场有着严格的秩序。也许正是因为此种秩序，诗人的创作诗思获得了最大的自由。

其二，自由的言说，自在的深思。

通过严谨的秩序而获得自由，其实是陆健常用的方式。通过对陆健诗歌创作的系统了解，我们就会发现，陆健对诗是一种形式化存在这一特征似乎早已心知肚明。和其他文体相比较，诗的形式化存在构成了这一文体的最基本特征，同时也是其本质特征。通过形式化呈现，使诗人和他的写作对象一起进入一种具有诗性的仪式性庆典活动之中。在这种诗性庆典活动——写作过程中，诗人和他的写作对象再也难以分出主客体的成分，再难分出诗人与诗。但是，当诗人与他的写作对象一旦走出这种仪式性庆典的"场"，他们就又成为一个普通凡人和普通的世事。按说，诗人在这种仪式性庆典的"场"中，其"思"的自由度与言说的时空关联应该是有限的。但《一位美轮美奂的小诗人之歌》却因其特定的有秩序的仪式性很强的形式建构而获得了极大的自由。而且，从整部诗集诗人所呈现出的创作情态来看，诗人的创作在这里不仅获得了极大自由，而且诗人在这里所呈现出的还是一种自在的言说。如果我们再认真观照一下诗人在这里呈现给我们的诗的主体内容，我们还会发现，诗人在诗中呈现给我们的是诗人、"小诗人"、历史与现实四维一体的主体时空。诗人与"小诗人"之间的自由转换，历史与现实之间的自由转换，中国与世界之间的自由转换，诗人用一部诗集给我们呈现出一个思想者自由自在的思想盛宴。诗人沉思的深刻与批判的犀利在当今的中国诗坛都是少有的。由于这部诗集的特殊建构使诗人的思想向度获得了极大的自由，因此，一部诗集中的每一组诗都像诗人呈现给我们的一幕幕思想的流星雨，自然天成且明亮瑰丽。这里，无法对诗集中的每一首诗做评述，我们只能举一两个例子感受一下诗人的诗思。陆健在其开篇《1 我对自己说吉约姆是你来的时候了——（法）吉约姆·阿波利奈》这首诗中所表明的是诗人对于"我"的认知。说实在的，对中国诗坛来说，自古至今，"我"都是一个问题。在中国的古典诗论中，有我之境和无我之境是没有高低贵贱之分的。从文人取诗的角度看，无我之境似乎更高超一些，这似乎与中国的诗歌审美大多取法于佛家的禅悟与道家的"道法自然""大道无形"有关，但"我"在中国古典诗歌中或隐或显，只是一个艺术境界的问题。尽管在"品"位上有人也区分其高下，但并不能构成一个多大的问题。如把其放在认知的领域来考察，也算是一个问题吧。"我"在诗歌中成为一个大问题，是新诗成为革命的工具之后，特别是二十世纪五十年代至八十年代之间，这时的诗歌，或者不能有个体的我的情感与思想，或者把我变成阶级的代言人。到了八十年代初，这个问题被作为新诗写作的障碍提出，于是，才有了"大写的我"这一观念。尽管是"大写的我"，"我"在诗中总算有了正当的名份。此后，由"大我"到"小我"，而后再把我的上半身去掉只留下半身写作，我终于与自己的机体建立起了联系。其实，自上世纪五十年代以降，"我"的问题对于中国诗人来说始终是个魔障，这对于每一个意在诗的创造性上有所作为的诗人来说都是一个不可忽视的问题。对此问题，在我看来，中国新诗坛上自始至终所有有关我的问题，都是一个关于"人"的问题。所有有关对于"我"的认识，说到底都是一个怎样认识"人"的问题。陆健在这部诗集的开篇，就是从寻找自我开始："我的天职是塑造一个当代诗人的形象/我必须千百次地打碎，塑造我自己/古往今来来过无数人……他们用话语堵住我的嘴巴。"尽管陆健在标题 A 中说"阿波利奈能来我当然也能"，但他进入诗思之后还是直面正视了这样一个问题：在那些"高大伟岸"的先贤面前，自己说话的权利还是没有多少余地。因此，在标题"a"六节诗里，陆健还是给"我"来了一次正名："我就是我，不是昨天的我/不是未来的我，不是一个概念，定义，是一个肉身。"在这首诗中，诗人为了呈现给我们一个真实实在的"我"，从用"阿波利奈能来我当然也能"展示出自己的野心到正视古往今来的贤哲用话语堵住"我"的嘴巴，再到对我是一个肉身的认知，再到食五谷，习文化，体认文明，再到直接宣示"我是暴政的敌人，同时又是一个温良的托尔斯泰主义者"。作者笔态恣肆，纵横古今中外，既表达了我与世界的关联，又在诗人灵智的归属上坚持了自己的民族立场，既展示了自我身上存在的矛盾，又对自己作为一个"生殖力旺盛"的"当代诗人"，"阿波利奈能来我当然也能"的意志品质给以了充分的体认。直面现实，直面自我，陆健的魅力，就是能够直面"我"是怎样一个人。在《2 我是无名小辈，你是谁？——（美）狄金森》这组诗里，陆健深刻反思了"我是谁更好些"这个"命题"。诗人通过"我"该成为"谁"这一设问，深刻地展示了在现代社会中"我"的丢失以及对自我追寻的迷惘与无助。"我是谁更好些"这一命题自身就是一出悲剧。我是谁都不会好，更不存在"更好些"这一问题。但是，当"我"是"谁"这一命题不能使"我"体现出"我"的实在之时，"我"就是"我"这一命题中的那个实在的真我又在哪里？对此，陆健在他的这部诗集里反反复复从诸多角度进行了反思。在《3 读书破万卷，下笔如有神——（中）杜甫》这组诗中，诗人在"C不是毛笔，也不是鹅毛笔"这个双重否定的陈述中，肯定了"我""在前贤止步的地方起笔"这个现代性的命题。如此的肯定实际上是标明了我们应该是处于一个"创世纪"的时代，但现实呢？"变声时期，一下子奔逃四散/谁也叫不出别人的名字。""丢失"是这个时代的通病，"城堡里骑士们在壁炉旁打牌/你叫一张里尔克，他甩一张德里达/维特根斯坦暂时在小 b 的手里占了上风/中国的太阳隔一层魔障，我们不小心/喜欢上了肯德基和家乐福的购物卡"。（《4 她恍若上界的一位天使，降临人间把奇迹向我们显示——（意）但丁》）陆健陈述的就是我们这个失去自我的时代的现实。中国文化诗性的丢失更是一件让人恐慌的事情。但在很多时候很多情况下，我们都是在自以为得意甚或是得意洋洋地自我丢失自我抛弃着。尽管诗人不无英雄主义地宣称："纵使世界已被拼贴成一张扁平的脸/诗人注定是那个挺身而出的鼻子"，但在今天这个世界里，诗人还是清醒地认识到，"如今商品的上帝要主宰她/诗歌为我们受尽凌迟之苦"。诗人生在这个世界上，或者更早些，或者更晚些，在很早很早以前，在遥远遥远的未来，但凡你是诗人，你必定要受尽炼狱之苦，这是诗人的宿命。如果这个世界不存在矛盾与痛苦，不存在丑恶与黑暗，这个世界就不需要诗人。诗与世俗世界，是一对矛盾，也是一个解不开的整体，诗与诗人不断被世俗绑架，又在不断地挣脱。诗人也就是在这个不断挣脱的过程中成就自己。或者死亡，或者重生。"谁已为我而死？我将为谁而死？"也许，我们并不清楚。"也许我穷尽一生完成了一个错误"，但是，"《苟余心之端直兮，虽僻远其何伤——（中）屈原》"。经历了《名城与门》，经历了《日内瓦的太阳》，经历了《温暖》，到今天《一位美轮美奂的小诗人之歌》，陆健的诗经由追寻人的现代性到探访人精神的远方，然后再回到人与土地的关系，直至今天全方位地展示人的问题这样一个历程，其实，始终都是在围绕一个目标，这个目标也就是人的问题。如果说陆健在早期的诗作中只是记录了人在现实世界的感受，比如，《美丽天真善良与悲剧》的悲剧，亦只不过是一种美丽的"冲突"，还无关人的命运，那么，到了《名城与门》《日内瓦的太阳》这个时期，陆健已在诗中探讨人类精神领域的宏阔空间以及人类在更为广袤的宇宙时空中的根本不幸。从某种意义上讲，这个时期，陆健对人与社会、人与宇宙的认识还是分离的，人就是人，世界就是世界。而到了《一位美轮美奂的小诗人之歌》，在诗人和这位美轮美奂的小诗人面前，人与这个世界就再也不能分开了，人就是这个世界的全部。这里，我们可以用陆健在这部诗集中几组诗的标题来串联一下，由此大体可以看出诗人的心灵时空以及诗人对人类命运的遥远思域：

《10 生存在你所生存的地方——（瑞典）古尔贝里》《11 每个人都应该对世上的一切人和一切事物负责——（俄）陀思妥耶夫斯基》《12，吾所以有大患者，为吾有身——（中）老子》《17 你选择什么样的存在，完全取决于自己——（法）萨特》《19 这世界就是舞台，可角色分配得不像样子——（英）王尔德》《20 我们只能享有我们所能理解的幸福——（比）梅特林克》，最终，人类只能感叹《26，天黑前路途遥遥，天黑前路途遥遥——（美）弗罗斯特》。在这些宏大的题目之下，陆健自然而然地给我们展示了诸多我们今天的细碎的生存场景：面粉，小米，肥壮的于坚，《老人与海》，越来越短的女人的裙子，微博，《道德经》，装嫩、装酷、装相、装死狗，儿子太小，春天太瘦，天牢囚徒，梁山毛贼，三鹿奶粉。高远的哲思与细碎的生存，都是我们，都是人自己和自己创造的一切，从细碎的生存再到对重大的民族命运的认识：

> 一百年来最伟大的汉语诗句
> "最危险的时候"，一个民族
> 对准了一首诗歌的腰部
>
> 最危险的时候，不在 1911 年
> 不在 1937、1946、1989 年
> 在今天，就在我们面前
>
> 就在于信仰倒地，道德狼藉
> 即使天才创造出崭新的文体
> 所有锦绣文章也只能是病句
>
> ——《15 中华民族到了最危险的时候——（中）田汉》

从对生活细节的细密感受到对民族命运的深广沉思，从幽默机趣的嘲讽调侃到正颜厉色的尖锐批判，这一切的一切，都构成了陆健诗歌中关乎人的元素。有趣的是，也就是在他处处思考着人的问题的时候，人这一概念却在他的诗中隐藏起来了，只留下一位美轮美奂的小诗人的歌唱。

2013.3.6 于郑州

单占生，河南文艺出版社总编辑，著名文学评论家。

中国当代诗坛的长篇杰作

——简论《一位美轮美奂的小诗人之歌》

熊国华

陆健的《一位美轮美奂的小诗人之歌》长达 783 行 10668 字，被诗人洪烛在网上誉为"最具震撼力的""2012 年我最喜欢的中国长诗"[1]。我以为考察一个时代的文化，首先应当考察诗人的境遇和水准。因为真正的诗人往往代表着时代的良知、民族的灵魂。陆健的《一位美轮美奂的小诗人之歌》以自身为研究个案，剖析了诗人在中国当代的境遇，以及由迷惘、焦虑、妥协、反思，到忏悔、抗争、担当、澄明的心灵历程，以讽喻的笔法给自己和当代诗人群体画像，也给我们这个物欲横流、光怪陆离的时代画像，用诗歌的刀锋切入诗人的心病和时代的癌症，其思想内涵的博大精深，以及在诗体形式上的探索创新，为长诗创作提供了一个新的成功范例，堪称中国当代诗坛的长篇杰作。

一

陆健在长诗的第一句即开宗明义——"我的天职是塑造一个当代诗人的形象"，全诗正是在这个基点上渐次展开。"我的主食是面粉、稻谷、玉米/儒家和道家的笔墨。通过翻译/品尝面包和西方文化的滋味"，这是中国诗人的日常生活方式和文化修养方式。"在他人面前把我的优点尽量放大/我是暴政的敌人，同时又是/一个温良的托尔斯泰主义者"，温良同时反对暴政，这是传统中庸土壤生长出来的中国文人性格。可见陆健在解剖自己的同时，也没有忘记显影中国当代知识分子和诗人群体的某些形象特征。

陆健以资深诗人的视角扫描了中国当代诗歌生态的"儒林外史":对文学大奖的渴望与嫉妒;模仿西方大师的翻译作品;微博时代写作的将错就错;消费时代诗歌被商品主宰的尴尬处境;迅速成名的葵花宝典;诗歌在烧酒、皮包、裤衩、卫生巾等广告商标上的"有用之用";从"追着那美腿,猛跑/从隐喻,到拒绝隐喻,到/下半身"的写作时尚,再到"把叙事叙到琐碎、琐碎不堪/把文化写到与文化无关的程度/把诗歌史写到遗忘了诗歌的程度"的极端病态,最后"诗歌的手臂已经脱臼/她扶不起那个叫做现实的大脑袋"。诗人淋漓尽致地披露诗界的种种怪现状,并不是呈一时口舌之快,而是为了指出诗歌存在的问题,寻找救治的良方,像当年的海德格尔一样发出"在今天的时代,诗人何为"的诘问!

具有担当精神的诗人首先拿自己开刀,作为自嘲或他嘲的讽刺对象,清理个人的生命历程和心灵垃圾,甚至不回避家庭隐私。"父亲在生我之前已经残废/留给我唯一的遗产就是原罪//我主要的培养基:母亲、舅舅、姨父/小知识分子、右派专家、公私合营/对象,他们默默一生无声响//我重要的营养液:大跃进、反右倾/三年自然灾害、文革十年风起云涌/以大有作为名义作一粒乡下的害虫"。而如今作为大学教授,"高兴时是傻子,痛苦时是诗人//执起教鞭把知识的营养与毒素/均匀搅拌,灌进学生食道,换回/我的柴米油盐和深深的愧疚"。他忏悔"自己有意或无意给别人的伤害""一次次/失信于自己,带上脸谱才出门去"的过往,并"记下我们对语言所犯的罪行"。在一个举世皆浊、众人皆醉的时代,"北京同样/需要有人站岗,看穿世界的心肠"。他决心"做回自己","保持与生俱来的善良木讷",走自己的路。既然不能像大诗人海涅一样"说出了天下最好的/名姓,也就说出了我的姓名"实现做大诗人的抱负,还不如听从博尔赫斯睿智的劝告"我的志愿就是做一个小诗人,而我已经达到"!在经历了一次次精神焦虑和灵魂历险之后,诗人顿悟人生,只有看破放下才能自在，步入暴风雨后的澄明之境。"我所有的仇恨都已经丢弃/妒能之心像荒年的米缸已经见底/……行走的人不会忘了亲爱的兄弟/我祝福他们，也没忘了自己"。既然赫尔博斯尚且如此，那我们就争取做"一群美轮美奂的小诗人"吧，坚守诗人的职责和良知，"为卑微的人们和自己写下诗章/轻声颂祷，麦花香和上天的垂顾""面对穹苍，俯察凡尘的面相/记录这岌岌可危的世界"，这才是诗人真正应当做的事情。

二

陆健用诗歌给自己画像，也给诗人群体画像，厘清了诗歌存在的诸多问题。其实，诗歌的问题和时代的问题就像藤和树的关系一样纠结在一起。诗人在给自己画像的同时，也有意无意地给我们所处的时代画了像。毕竟不愧是国家传媒大学的教授，毕竟一不小心活了半个多世纪，而且走南闯北阅人无数，陆健在这部长诗中给我们展现了近乎包罗万象、繁复驳杂的时代景观。其内容涉及历史、文化、科学、宗教、哲学、文学、伦理、政治、经济、教育、体育、医学、建筑、民俗、烹饪、娱乐、婚姻、爱情等各个领域，而且生活细节和场面十分丰富。诗人穿越时空，融汇中西，从古埃及的《亡灵书》、希腊的荷马史诗，写到中国的老子、孔子；从原始人类的狩猎，写到现代高科技；从市井百姓写到奥巴马等国家元首，以及我们所处时代光怪陆离的现象。笔锋所指之处，让人感到"见血封喉"的力度。

诸如："人类在伊甸园中获得的第一个权利/是隐私权"，而现在人们反文化就首先反对隐私权，"研究文化，就频频意淫/成人保健用品呼啸在乡镇，网站/裸聊，夏装露出脐部及两瓣后臀"。诸如文化时尚的炒作，"学术秀、真人秀、做秀、模仿秀/口齿伶俐秀、结结巴巴秀""装嫩、装酷、装相、装死狗"，令人哭笑不得！诸如责任感的流失，"上午我挂号之后，医生要我对肚子里/莫须有的囊肿负责，而他只对医院/的收费处负责。黄昏的公园角落里她/抽抽搭搭地，恋爱已经无法向处女负责"。诸如社会诚信和道德的丧失,"当年野合的恋人正喊着开房/听收割机的响动,吃撑了农药的/麦苗噌噌地长,通向城市的道路//加油站收费站林立,歌星的体型/膨胀,大过整个广场的假唱/楼角转出整容后的邻居女郎"。忧国忧民的诗人为民请命,大声疾呼"解散突发事件办公室,减少税负/减少警察和城管、环境污染之虞,让/薪水坐上行电梯,物价坐下行电梯"。他尖锐地指出中华民族"最危险的时候……就在于信仰倒地,道德狼藉"!他从生态整体主义的立场出发,深刻指出"人类像疯长的野草//没有给地球带来多少价值意义/一群人的荣耀,是另一群人的/毒药"。

毫无疑问,诗人以深刻精确的描述给我们所处的时代弊病做了一个全方位的"心电图"。这种综合概括生活的能力不是一般"小诗人"所能达到的。长诗无论在表现时代生活的深度和广度,还是在批判丑恶现象的力度等方面都不同凡响,具有一种震撼心灵的力量。诗人在披露时代痼疾的过程中同时也在思考——我在这个时代做了什么,如何才能拯救人类?诗人上下求索,最后找到的良方是"爱":"能够包围一座城池的,是爱/能够包围整个地球的,只能是爱","像耶稣说的无所不在,胜过//汽车、电脑、导弹,胜过宇宙飞船/胜过一万年所有的科学的钢铁花朵/和显微镜下人造干细胞的精密技术"。爱能化解仇恨、救赎灵魂、创造美好!"把爱接通到人心里去,以免缺血/紊乱、梗死"。他大胆呼吁"政府如果无法让爱像/货币一样流通,它就该天天给自己放假"!他继承了李白蔑视权贵的遗风,"当今的伟大人物,就像被孩子/用草帽扣住的那只蚂蚱""伟大只是穿行于人间的风"。如果不能造福于人类造福于地球,谈何伟大?他像崇尚爱的哲学一样崇尚自然,崇尚淡泊名利的隐士,"我要用文学史的完整一章来谈陶潜/在王府井大街背诵桃花源/让天底下的人物植物都听见"。这确实是一位可敬可爱的"美轮美奂的小诗人"!

三

如上所述，这部长诗的时空跨度极大，内容几乎包括社会生活的各个领域。用何种形式来承载如此庞大沉重的内容，这是长诗作者必须考虑的一个关系作品成败的问题。诗歌从文体形式来说，长于抒情而短于叙事。以往的长诗大多是描写一个人物、一个故事，或者歌颂一个党派、一个国家。结构多呈线性发展，比较简明单调。因其叙事成分太多，语言也比较直白而缺乏诗味。这种传统的长诗结构和写法，用来抒写现代生活的繁复喧嚣和现代人心理感受的微妙复杂，无疑是难以胜任的。《一位美轮美奂的小诗人之歌》在诗体建设上勇于创新，为长诗创作提供了一个可供参考的成功范例。

这部长诗的结构极为独特，按 26 字个英文字母分为 26 章，但却用阿拉伯数字 1 至 26 标号排列，诗句均用汉字书写。每一章下又有 2 个标题，分别为英文字母的大写和小写作为序号。全诗均为 3 行一节，大写序下为 3 节，小写序下为 6 节，即每一章都是 9 节 27 行诗，结构严谨有序。笔者不太清楚陆健为什么恰恰是写了 26 章，正如笔者不太清楚英文 26 个字母的具体来历和含义。但是有一点可以肯定：所有英文都是由 26 个字母拼写出来的，26 个字母自成一个语言符号体系。由此，我们是否可以窥探陆健的诗心，即这部长诗的 26 章也是自身具足、自成体系的（分则独立成章，合则形成整体），而且寓有融合中西、包罗万象之意。这是其一。

其二，英文字母的大写和小写及所属内容，类似音乐的主调与复调，暗藏玄机。在欧洲中世纪的宗教音乐以单声调的主调音乐为主，文艺复兴时期神性消减，人性复苏，逐渐引进世俗音乐。至巴洛克时期的德国伟大的音乐家巴赫，大量创作了复调音乐，两个或两个以上的旋律"同时进行而组成相互关连的有机整体。在横的关系上，各声部在节奏、重音、力度、起迄以及旋律线的起伏等方面各有其独立性；在纵的关系上，各声部又彼此形成和声关系。复调音乐以对位法为其主要创作技法"[2]。在陆健的长诗中，大写字母标题类似主调，小写字母标题类似复调；一般情况下大写代表精神生活，小写代表世俗生活。在当今时代大众文化占据优势，所以小写字母下的诗句比大写字母下的诗句数量多一倍。精神、精英思想与世俗、大众思想相互渗透、交叉融合，以此对应多元复杂的社会生活现象。

其三，每一章的大标题与属下的大写字母、小写字母标题，形成一种互文关系。大标题全部都是引用古今中外的名人名言、或名诗名句，在一章中起到提纲挈领的作用。"这是发出的一声呼唤或是唤起一段回忆，交流如此建立：所有的作品，全部的文学宝库被简约地回顾，和我的作品一道在读者的脑中交织"[3]，引导读者跟随诗人的思路进入一个崭新的艺术空间。每一章内的英文大写和小写标题，一般是从承接大标题的指向而展开的抒写、延伸和诠释。大写标题及序下内容比较精神、概括、虚一点，小写标题及序下内容比较世俗、具体、实一点。楼梯式的三级标题及内涵互相对应、交织、激发、转喻、诠释、扩散，形成一种多重感应的互文关系的语义场，类似多声部的旋律同时发声并且彼此融洽对位形成的和声。

其四，全诗每一节均为 3 行诗句，在长诗建行上极为罕见。无论新诗还是古诗，4 句（行）一节的形式沿用已久，且为人们所熟悉。唐代形成的近体诗，绝句为标准的 4 句，律诗 8 句 4 联仍可以说是变相的 4 句，起承转合的形式成为一种思维定式，严谨整齐的格律，实际上是长期农耕文明四季变化、稳定生活的的一种心理反映。以商品和信息为标志的现代生活瞬息万变，天灾人祸防不胜防，城市人群心理上的压力、焦虑、浮躁和欲望早已消解了田园牧歌式的情调。在一个无法奢谈心理稳定的时代，诗人通过自我强化的意志竭力寻求一种内心的定力，并把这定力外化为一种虽不稳定但又要勉力为之的形式秩序，化偶为奇 3 行成节，也许是一种较好的选择，即冲破了 4 句成节的思维定势，又建立了一种新的形式秩序。虽然 3 行成节在新诗中已经有不少人运用,但一部洋洋万言的长诗从始至终都是3行成节却是罕见的,说是一种创造性的运用也似无不可。举例说明如下:

8. 我悲哀地看着我们这一代人——(俄)莱蒙托夫

H. 我们这一代人悲哀地看着莱蒙托夫
学术秀、真人秀、做秀、模仿秀
口齿伶俐秀、结结巴巴秀。作
沉思状、作假想状荒诞状、作

左半身右半身极不对称状
装嫩、装酷、装相、装死狗
你扎它一下,它就逾墙走

我被襁褓生出来而非从母体出世
我的智慧来自真理而非来自生活
我们这一代人悲哀地看着莱蒙托夫

h. 迅速成名的葵花宝典
甲、给自己起一个别致的笔名
假如一位上海诗人,最好叫外白
与他唱和的女友恰如其分地名叫渡桥

乙、借助名校,把诗歌运动起来
热热闹闹,自己的名字活色生香
出现在大刊小报及各种选本之中

丙、官方民间两不得罪。诗坛已呈颓势

在污染物与杂草之间穿行，将来做大时
再以春秋笔法进行外科手术式的批评

丁、学外语。说得跟跟跄跄没关系
写诗清一色欧式句子，便于翻译
最好找李笠直接捎到斯德哥尔摩去

戊、站在煊赫有力的魁梧身形旁边
人们在看见他们的同时看见了我
在看见刺绣品的同时看到了针线

己、作死了个别名人的对立面
当然以无辜者的面目出现。而且
胆大包天的成功者心是比针尖还细的

长诗第 8 章的标题，引用俄国作家莱蒙托夫的名言"我悲哀地
看着我们这一代人"。英文第 8 个字母大写 H 标题"我们这一代人悲
哀地看着莱蒙托夫"，是从大标题引申而出，并反其意而用之；所属
9 行诗句，对我们时代流行的作秀炒作现象进行了嘲讽，矫揉造作弄
虚作假，真相被歪曲遮蔽而本末倒置，所以"我们这一代人悲哀地看
着莱蒙托夫"，与大标题形成互文关系，但内容比较抽象、概括、"精
神"。小写英文字母 h 标题"迅速成名的葵花宝典"，借用金庸小说
《笑傲江湖》中武功秘籍《葵花宝典》来讽刺当代诗坛迅速成名的各
种伎俩，比较具体、丰富、"世俗"，与大写 H 标题形成对位复调，是
对追逐名利不择手段行为的进一步披露、诠释和反讽，凸显了我们这
一代人文化精神上的悲哀，同时又与大标题形成回应的互文关系。三
重标题的并置构成了诗歌的多重结构、多维时空和多元对话，打破了
历史与现实、时间与空间、东方与西方的界限，把个体行为放到一个

极为广阔的时代、历史语境中去考察评价，其内涵比单一标题更为丰富深厚。3 行一节的形式，突破了 4 行一节的思维定式，给人简洁、清晰、新颖的感觉。3 行在意义上可以独立成节，也可以利用断句把 2 节串连在一起（如上例的第 1 节和第 2 节），承接和转换比 4 行一节更为灵活自由。虽然长诗不是所有的章节都按照以上模式写作，但适当的离散、易位和变化，反而能使篇章结构更为丰富多彩，符合整齐而有变化的美学原则。

陆健以诗人的良知、对真理的追求和卢梭式的忏悔精神抒写了《一位美轮美奂的小诗人之歌》，其思想内涵的博大精深，对现实生活的关注与批判，对人与自然、社会关系的探求，以及对存在意义、人类命运的追寻和考问，给我们带来诸多有益的启示和心灵震撼。在诗歌与人、人与时代的思考中，他勇于探索实验，殚精竭虑地寻找相应的表现形式，终于创造了一个体大思精、严谨奇妙的长诗结构，实现了自己多年的诗学梦想。"纵使世界已被拼贴成一张扁平的脸／诗人注定是那个挺身而出的鼻子"，我们记住了陆健给自己和时代的绝妙画像。

参考文献：

[1]洪烛《2012 年度我最喜欢的中国长诗》，
http://blog.sina.com.cn/hongzhublog

[2]《辞海·艺术分册》，上海辞书出版社 1980 年版，第 137 页。

[3]瓦勒里·拉尔堡《承蒙圣·热罗姆之庇佑》，见（法）蒂费纳·萨莫瓦约著、邵炜译《互文性研究》，天津人民出版社 2003 年版，第 35 页。

2013 年 3 月 18 日

熊国华，广东第二师范学院中文系主任、教授，海外华文文学研究所所长，国际诗人笔会秘书长。

心灵荒原的"但丁式"拷问与救赎

——陆健长诗《一位美轮美奂的小诗人之歌》论稿

子 午

"乾坤浮一气，今古浸双丸。"（张照《观海》）诗歌是一个时代语言和良知的制高点，是思想与审美海拔的文本雕塑，是一个民族心灵史最本质、简练而灵动的真实写照。

陆健说："我的左手握住诗歌，右手抓住现实"（见长诗第三章）。自 90 年代初迄今的 20 多年间，他积极探索汉语诗歌的诗体建设、体裁及其艺术形式的多样性和可能性，并取得了可喜的实质性突破。早在 1992 年 9 月，陆健的诗集《名城与门》在文化艺术出版社问世后，笔者就曾指出：陆健创造了一种新的体裁：诗特写（Poetry feature）。其后的《34 份礼物》（2004 年 5 月）也是诗特写的成功之作。而《非典时期的了了特特博士》（2003 年 6 月）、《枫叶上的比尔》（2006 年 6 月）、《田楼，田楼》（2006 年 10 月）和《洛水之阳》（2007 年 4 月）等诗集的艺术形式及其风格则属纪实诗（Documentary poetry）[1]。毫不夸张地说，陆健的诗特写和纪实诗系列创作在中国新诗史上均具有开创性及建设意义。

前不久，陆健创作的长诗《一位美轮美奂的小诗人之歌》（见 2013 年 3 期《中国诗歌》）堪称中国当代的经典长诗。在诗中，他借鉴了但丁《神曲》的长诗结构及其若干艺术元素，并以艾略特式的敏锐、深刻和恢宏，从新诗建设的立场及诗人的自省精神出发，通过自我拷问一步步走向并展开对整个社会普遍存在的"心灵荒原"的拷问。应当指出，这部璀璨、绚丽的长诗既是中国当代诗坛的一个缩影，更是现代社会人们心灵现实的最直接的反映。

一、结构：借《神曲》之形，融赋格之魂

（从疗救诗歌到对文化的救赎）

从结构上看，陆健的《一位美轮美奂的小诗人之歌》一方面借鉴了但丁《神曲》的"宏大叙事"结构之"神"，另一方面则化用了由字母和严密数字逻辑矩阵所组成的数学之"形"。长诗共 26 章，每章分为两首（也可视为类似中国古典诗歌的上、下两阕），依次用 26 个大、小写英文字母作为序号。其中，每章上阕均为 3 小节共 9 行，下阕为 6 小节共 18 行（即每章共 27 行），全诗共 702 行（不包括大、小标题）。诗人匠心独运地用类似音乐的对位法来结构全诗，整部长诗犹似一部结构严谨、风格唯美的赋格[2]体交响乐或精湛别致的歌剧。

长诗一起笔就直奔中心。一如但丁在《神曲·地狱篇》中遇到的第一个人是古罗马时期的伟大诗人维吉尔（他引领但丁游历了地狱和炼狱），陆健在其长诗的第一章遇到的则是法国诗人、小说家、评论家、剧作家阿波利奈[3]（他对立体主义、未来主义、达达主义和超现实主义等文艺领域的先锋运动影响尤为深远）。陆健把阿波利奈放在长诗里 20 多位中外文化名人的首位，是蕴含深意的。他希望自己能从阿波利奈身上汲取开拓创新的智慧和力量。在长诗开篇的第一首，陆健用带有《诗经》赋体诗传统的笔调开宗明义地写道："我的天职是塑造一个当代诗人的形象/我必须千百次地打碎、塑造我自己"。

当新诗潮运动在 80 年代末结束以来，陆健一直苦苦思考，呕心沥血地探索中国新诗的出路。他以一个学者型诗人独有的敏锐，洞见了中国诗坛（乃至整个文坛）一度出现的思想浮躁疲软，文化上缺乏深层历练，因而游戏文学和消费语言，并导致诗歌的低媚倾向（如低

诗写作、下半身写作）及网络语言泛滥等现象。对此，陆健就像一个诗歌"先知"般体会得格外深入。"哦诗歌//过去道德的上帝盯上了她/如今商品的上帝要主宰她/诗歌为我们受尽凌迟之苦"（长诗第六章）。

陆健的生活及其诗歌写作历程真实地折射出中国诗人族群的总体精神风貌。他在诗中自我调侃地写道："我知道自己仍然是个小人物//儿时为长大而吃饱穿暖；然后下身/与智力一同胀大。饱读杂书，用/手指和键盘的相互取悦代替书写"。"常常类乎抄袭，偶尔灵光闪现"。他非常理智地将自己定位于"在前贤止步的地方起笔/从波德莱尔以来便是如此"（长诗第三章）；尽管我们"已有的其它写作，无论如何勤勉/除了练笔功能，全是无效劳动"（长诗第十三章）。

他毫不犹豫地以解剖刀式的思辩语言揳入当代诗坛，为当下的诗歌现状诊病："诗坛已呈褪势/在污染物与杂草之间穿行"（长诗第八章）。事实上，以陆健为代表的优秀诗人已责无旁贷地接力肩起"五四"时期的启蒙重任（既是诗的启蒙，也是人性和文化的启蒙）。"荒凉在我眼里"，他这时内心的感受就像"还没出道的勇士一般"（长诗第十章）。

而最让我们感到震撼的，是陆健对现代人普遍存在的心灵"荒漠化"图景的描述。从信息传播的意义上说，网络传媒的发展一方面是文化的推进器，促进了"信息高速公路"的形成；另一方面它始料未及地却成了信息复制、情感复制，甚至是文化复制的温床，并由此导致了以下两个后果：一是原创性文化产品越来越少，二是它又反过来对文化、信息自身进行消解。于是，信息复制→信息过剩→思想枯竭，成了一种恶性循环的"信息消解"（思想消解）流程。

1．信息复制：科技＝保鲜？

透过陆健的诗句，我们隐约感觉到他那语言的锋刃上所闪射出来的寒光。"我们这一代人悲哀地看着莱蒙托夫"。这寒光——从现代人眼里和语境里的"荒凉"直指心灵的"荒原"。"我伸出手来，是要索取，还是/送给别人他所需要的东西？"（长诗第十章）难道说，"科学技术的聪明发明了冰箱/它（的作用仅仅是）要为陈旧的故事保持新鲜"（长诗第五章）？

陆健在长诗的第二章，借美国传奇女诗人埃米莉·伊丽莎白·狄金森之口说："我是无名之辈，你是谁？"在信息被一再复制的时代，诗人每天"在闪念间，在被虫子蠹空的日历里/在籍，在册，在人群中蹀躞而行"。而我们所能做的，就是在这"天苍苍野茫茫"中，以一种置身物外的方式进行自我保鲜——以"活个洒脱通透"（长诗第十章），这无疑已成了我们唯一的"选择"。

紧接着，陆健将形而上的哲学命题不着墨痕地转入生存层面的具体细节的叙写："可是儿子太小，春天太瘦"；"我眼观工资条：一是一二是二/我周边，缺少阔大而粗砺的自然"（同上）。这便是这一代人（包括诗人）的共同命运。也许可以称之为"命运的复制"（或保鲜）。既要从为人夫、为人父（还有为人子）等的角色中担当着养家活口的生活艰辛，更得肩负起文化和人性启蒙及新诗建设的时代使命。而要完成这两项重任，惟有一再地对频繁转型的网络语境及诗歌语言进行"科技保鲜"。因为青年诗人的更新换代和网络语言的淘汰率太快了，比流行乐坛的歌手淘汰速度还要快。

A. 语言复制：名词与蛀牙　网络时代的人们已习惯在程序化、符号化的环境中生活，当语言、信息被一再复制和互相复制，词汇也自然而然地成了一种面具。面对这一现象，陆健用他惯有的幽默语调从容写道——

"其实唐朝，李白还是李黑，又有
什么区别呢？高行健是法国人

还是中国人，又有什么关系呢？"

（长诗第二章）

从什么时候起，人们就开始热衷于"拼命给语言吃糖，把名词牙蛀掉//甚至给笔下的事物隆胸，嫁接、拼凑/生造、割裂概念，如同超市的/'火烧冰激凌'"（同上）。生活的虚假导致语言的失真和面具化，而语言的虚假则直接导致诗歌对生活的失真及悖逆。

B. 情感复制：道和理→同性恋？　现实中很多事物表面上看似没有什么关联，而实际上凡是共存于这个世界的所有事物都存在着内在的关联。美国气象学家爱德华·罗伦兹早在1963年就发现了这一混沌学的"蝴蝶效应"[4]现象。他提出了这样一个著名的命题："一只南美洲亚马逊河流域热带雨林中的蝴蝶，偶尔扇动几下翅膀，可以在两周以后引起美国德克萨斯州的一场龙卷风。"据说这一效应理论便是受到2200多年前"庄周梦蝶"的启发。

同样地，陆健也是受到了《庄子·齐物论》里"不知周之梦为蝴蝶与？蝴蝶之梦为周与"的启发。在日常生活中，"国家""人民"等使用频率最高的字眼常常沦为被盗用最多的词汇。这是一种关于集合概念的不约而同的集体情感复制行为。"比如国与家//这两个词汇，从泾渭分明到模糊不清/比如道和理，竟成了同性恋关系/伊人在水一方，如今滚成一团"（长诗第九章）。

陆健最擅于在诗中将严肃的茎叶连接上一个个幽默的花蕾。甚至，他把人的情感信息复制与同性恋问题粘贴到一块（据世卫组织的权威统计比值，在100个人中有4～6人为同性恋者）。"'煤球是黑的'和'元宵是白的'/都对，但都自说自话，却没提/它们都是圆的。"（长诗第十七章）。陆健的幽默就这样"润物细无声"地渗透到每个诗句和每个词象建筑中。

2. 信息垃圾：过剩/话语遮蔽

毫无疑问，哲学问题的验证最终总得归结到数学方法论层面上去。同样地，陆健在描述置身于信息过剩的语境感受时，他也用数字量化的方式来表示："我吃了一千碗饭，为伦勃朗的绘画/镶上一幅铝合金的画框；我洗了/一百次澡，濡湿黄宾虹的狼毫"（长诗第七章）。而最具有反讽意义的，人类文明就是通过这样一种方式痛并快乐着——

"八大山人的鸟鸣刚被听见
艾略特就在他的黄昏里昏过去了

博尔特比鲍威尔提高了 0.16 秒
哲学家回过头去研究老子的高妙
我的书案摊开《道德经》17 个版本"
（同上）

信息过剩导致垃圾信息（包括垃圾诗、垃圾文化）的大量产生，"语言成了喘息/韵脚成了垃圾，翻滚着，弥漫着"（长诗第十五章）；"一二三四五六七/数字发声之后变成物质之欲"，并"把叙事叙到琐碎、琐碎不堪/把文化写到与文化无关的程度/把诗歌史写到遗忘了诗歌的程度"（长诗第十六章）。

"与文化无关""遗忘诗歌"不但是对文化和诗歌的遮蔽，同时更是文化传播者及诗人的一种自我遮蔽。这也许是他们在传播文化和写作诗歌时所始料未及的。成千上万的信息当它甫一发出便已在半途上被淹没和"格式化"了。当一个话语场在生成的同时，它立刻就被一个更为巨大的隐形的场、秩序所遮蔽（包括各个话语体系之间的相互遮蔽）。

3．思想枯竭：心灵"荒原"的形成

整整一代人表现在个体思想的迷惘、荒芜和心灵枯竭，不可避免地导致现代人心灵"荒原"的形成。一如艾略特从"看进光的中心，那一片沉寂"，进而看到了整个社会"荒凉而空虚是那大海"（艾略特《荒原》第一章《死者的葬礼》）。艾略特在这部长诗中，让荒原同波德莱尔笔下的巴黎和但丁笔下的地狱作对比，并将神话的、人类学的、基督教的和东方宗教的意象结合在一起，着重描写了冬天早晨黑雾下的伦敦景象：一座虚幻的城。以此反映和象征第一次世界大战后整个西方世界的精神危机。艾略特在90年前对伦敦景象的描写（《荒原》写于1919～1922年间，1922年10月在文学刊物《标准》上发表），竟不幸成为当下现代人心灵"荒原"的一种预言式折射。

这就是信息化时代每天上演的严峻的语言现实和文化现实。陆健同样以艾略特的"荒原"意识及其诗性智慧观照了中国当代诗坛乃至在同一语境下的整个现代社会。当他从现代人的心灵"荒漠"中瞥见了："花朵已无力保护它的花香，罂粟的美/决定了她必须躲躲藏藏，长髯飘飘的/拉琴者最后拉断了自己的脖子"（长诗第九章）；陆健也禁不住发出了沉重而无奈的喟叹——因为"博尔赫斯已为光明/失去了他那有洞察力的眼睛"，"士兵已为将军而死，生命已为棺木而死"（长诗第六章）。

据此，陆健考之有据地指出当代诗歌的病理所在："诗人应该向字、词的皮癣负责/语言的脾胃不适，它摄取的营养单一/以致骨质疏松[5]，体质时常虚弱"（长诗第十一章）。现代人的"心灵体质"就是这样从字词到脾胃，再到骨组织，一步步逐渐陷入"荒漠化"的。

从诗歌的内在精神层面上说，陆健诗中所表现的现代人"心灵荒原"一如但丁的《神曲》"地狱篇"（共九层地狱）所描写的灵肉煎熬情景及其总体象征。从长诗的结构上说，从《第一章　我对自己说吉约姆是你来的时候了（吉约姆·阿波利奈）》至《第八章　我悲哀

地看着我们这一代人（莱蒙托夫）》，相当于《神曲》的"地狱篇"；从《第九章　苟余心之端直兮，虽僻远其何伤？（屈原）》至《第十七章　你选择什么样的存在，完全取决于自己（萨特）》，相当于《神曲》的"炼狱篇"；那么，从《第十八章　断竹，续竹，飞土，逐肉（上古歌谣·弹歌）》至《第二十六章　天黑前路途遥遥，天黑前路途遥遥（弗罗斯特）》，则相当于《神曲》的"天堂篇"（仅就章节结构而言）。

　　不用讳言，虽然长诗在这一部分并没有表现与《神曲》相对应的"天堂"生活内容（陆健仅仅是通过诗的方式提出问题，而作为一个诗人及其诗歌作品本身是不具备也没有必要为全社会的人性救赎和文化救赎直接担责的），人类文明发展至今到底有没有人性与文化的"天堂"，这永远是一个了无尽头的"斯芬克斯"之谜；但是，陆健在这里却不无庆幸地选择了山东日照的女孩君娜作为自己的"贝阿特丽切"[6]。"她恍若上界的一位天使，降临人间把奇迹向我们显示。"（但丁）恰恰是这个君娜，她"要用自己的虔诚之心／证明所有人都是弥足珍贵的"；与此同时，她更使诗人陆健感到面前的"世界就不同以往"，于是他"不再疑惑于诗，于美丽／太太碰碰我，说你是不是爱上她了？／我想了想，答'是'。"（长诗第十八章）

　　随着陆健的笔端，他审视的目光从古代、近代写到当代，由诗歌写到社会，自中国写到世界，写出了整整一个时代的人们在高科技和商业化语境下逐渐物化、纯化和麻木的心灵图景。当"时间的吊臂摆动，也许历史在前／未来在后，也许是它的反面／也许我穷尽一生完成一个错误"（长诗第七章）；而作为一个有着知识分子历史使命的诗人，陆健更加清醒地看到——

　　"意识形态螺旋上升，民族、国家、主义
　　流派和诗歌的本质、原则、手法。我的

手掌上的纹理，也是假借了自由的名义"

（同上）

至此，陆健给中国诗歌（乃至整个文坛）开出了一个建议性的救赎"良方"——既是对诗歌的救赎，也是对文化的救赎，更是对现代人的心灵的救赎："文字和人类一样，需要放血疗法/诗歌的斧头砍上去，它流血/它流血的同时我倒下，借助灰土的传扬"（同上）。正是通过这一文化"放血"、语言"放血"和思想"放血"，才能真正达到自我救赎之目的。

二、词象秩序：传统基因与文化宿命

（从自我拷问到对一代人的拷问）

在这部长诗中，陆健从一代人的缩影延伸出去，写尽了人生的悲喜沉浮和苍凉。"挑开事件，看到我们的人生/我们苍茫、苍白或仓皇的人生//这是被命运指定的内容，因此/我们时而被自己或别人的笔触感动/命运，它的大小就是我们的大小"（长诗第十三章）。

1．绕不开的家族密码：农耕文明＋儒道笔墨

陆健在诗中有时冷静得让人吃惊！一方面他勇于正视并坦承自身对传统的承传关系（民族元素与文化元素等），坦承这代人的某种先天不足，乃至营养不良；另一方面他又不得不以一种自我解嘲的口吻说：我"不是一个/概念、定义，是一个肉身"，虽然有人"说我长着一个铁制的头颅/木制的躯干与双手，泥坯/堆成的腿脚"（长诗第一章）。

我们每个人身上都带有这一共同的家族密码，带有它的谱系元素、惯性及无奈。"我忽而巨大忽而渺小，少不经事/四十而惑，五十不知天命，活着/活着就把自己活成了这个样子"（长诗第二章）。

在中国当代诗坛，从来没有一个诗人和诗评家能像陆健这样，俨

然一个有着良好医德的医生（对了，他是正宗清皇室御医之后），亲切、冷静并负责任地把这代人的社会构成成分、文化质地、语言能力和几千年的农耕传统背景梳理得如此清晰和准确无误。而且是用诗的方式和诗的语言来完成的——

> "我的主食是面粉、稻谷、玉米
> 儒家和道家的笔墨。通过翻译
> 品尝面包和西方文化的滋味
>
> 我是农耕文明的产物，被机器
> 快速裹挟，一头扎进计算机里
> 小心翼翼，护住自己的软肋
>
> 在他人面前把我的优点尽量放大
> 我是暴政的敌人，同时又是
> 一个温良的托尔斯泰主义者"
> （长诗第一章，同上）

中华民族几千年的文化基因早已深深地融入每个后来者（包括诗人）身上。一如陆健所归纳的：我们的家族密码"主食是面粉、稻谷、玉米""儒家和道家的笔墨"。"通过翻译"，我们才能"品尝面包和西方文化的滋味"。我们是"农耕文明的产物"，"被机器/快速裹挟，一头扎进计算机里/小心翼翼，护住自己的软肋"。陆健的描述惟妙惟肖，令人叫绝！

2. 诗与生活及与诗人的距离：语言关系

诗与生活的距离从来就是检验一首诗、一个诗人是否重要、是否有价值的主要依据。那么，"一首诗能引导我们走多远。或者/说，我们距离一首诗多远"？陆健清醒地看到："总觉得《诗经》《橘颂》的作者/在嘲讽今日的写家。其实《诗经》作者/没功夫挑刺，他们只是钟爱名词"（长诗第五章）。

不消说，陆健在诗史及诗歌美学的视野上是明智的。用一句北京话说，其实陆健心里早就像明镜儿似的。他不但对诗与生活的关系看得透彻，而且对诗与诗人的关系也把握得准确到位，恰到好处。他从对古典诗歌的考察和梳理中得到了有益启示。"至唐代诗人——文采风流，像一群/勤快的丫鬟给小姐梳头，刮腻子擦粉/用形容词把诗歌的品相打磨装修//细致到几乎遭小姐烦的程度。后世/的才子们似乎得到要领，当仁不让"（同上）。陆健的幽默常常使人忍俊不禁。

被奉为中国诗歌经典的唐诗中尚且有"做"和"隔"之嫌，那么，在当下网络时代的诗歌"复制"式作坊里，诗与诗人的距离更是变得暧昧和不可捉摸，有时仿若咫尺天涯，有时则接近"零"（被称为零摩擦、零距离，于是出现了零度叙事，和于坚的《零档案》等等）。这样一来，就连心里像明镜儿似的陆健有时也显得有点无奈："我知道自己在做什么"，但同时"我（又）不知道/自己在做什么。"（长诗第二章）实际上，诗与诗人的关系最终归结为一种语言关系（陆健将这一诗歌生成关系称为"语言的扮相"，并作为长诗第九章下阕的标题）。

A. 物理（身体）距离：原罪+培养基　在陆健的长诗中，物理距离的语言长度是通过身体（肉身）来体现的。《老子·十三章》说："吾所以有大患者，为吾有身；及吾无身，吾有何患？"意思是说：我们之所以有忧患，是因为我们有自我的存在；如果我们忘掉自我，我们还有什么忧患的呢？这里的所谓"无身"，实质是指"无我"境界。人一旦达到无我境界，就没有什么忧患了。

事实上肉身距离就是一种现实距离。它既是时间形态，也是空间形态。诗人洪烛曾经说过："与其说世界是由物质构成的，莫如说是由形形色色的词语构成的。词已成为物的替身。"

"一个孱弱的精子是我的前身

我父亲在生我之前已经残废

留给我唯一的遗产就是原罪

我主要的培养基：母亲、舅舅、姨父

小知识分子、右派专家、公私合营

对象，他们默默一生无声响"

（长诗第十二章）

在这里，"一个孱弱的精子"表明这代人的先天不足；"原罪"实质是指这代人的共同命运："我重要的营养液：大跃进、反右倾/三年自然灾害、文革十年风起云涌/以大有作为名义作一粒乡下的害虫"（长诗第十二章）。

陆健的"自省式"真诚差不多已抵近法国伟大的启蒙思想家、哲学家和作家卢梭的"忏悔式"真诚。他在诗中毫不留情地把自己及同代人的"家族身世"进行史学和人文科学层面的披露及剖析。

B. 心理距离：傻子+诗人　陆健的可贵之处在于，他不但对本民族历史悠久、源远流长的文化传统和诗学传统了然在心，而且，他对这一文化的构成和汉语诗歌的特定文化基因、时代元素与语言积淀也研究得相当透彻。这正是成就大诗和经典诗歌的前提条件。

陆健坦承：这些与物质世界共存互生的"语言生物"（使用母语写诗的人），"高兴时是傻子，痛苦时是诗人"（长诗第十三章）。正所谓"历史创造英雄，英雄也创造历史"。而所有的历史都挥不开战争、饥饿的影子及动力。请看陆健笔下的这一代人——

"睁着饿得发绿、瞳孔放大的双眼

我惧怕所有人，仇视一切人

在梦遗里忙于亵渎美丽的女性

若不是又有了书读，我早就成了

天牢囚徒、梁山毛贼，五脏六腑

把那一带的好人好事全消化干净"

（长诗第十二章）

陆健甚至借诗中抒情主体（潜在主人公）之口说："我细瘦的书生之手，也能见血封喉"

（同上）。其实，中外历史往往是由一群时而傻、时而疯的人所推动的。据世卫组织统计，在全球 70 亿人中，超过六成人患有程度不等的心理疾患。其中有相当一部分人会在后天自愈。这就是说，人类的各个阶层和行业中都会产生心理不健康的人及疯子。而政治家这一高风险、玩权谋的人群尤甚。据《纽约时报》报道，美国杜克大学医学中心的乔纳森·戴维森博士、凯瑟琳·康纳博士和马文·斯瓦兹等三位精神病学家，通过大量的材料研究发现，从 1789 年到 1974 年间，近半数的美国总统（高达 37 位）在其生命的某个阶段曾患过不同程度的精神疾病。

C. 词象距离：残缺的美　在词与象之间、在语言与诗之间，象的距离实际上也是的人心理距离。"一顶桂冠从一个荷马头上，转移到/另一个荷马头上。他自己是看不见这/桂冠的，他看见的是自己内心的黑暗"（长诗第二章）。一如杜甫，他的落点"总在古典主义界内"。

陆健说："极端事物无不有美潜隐/其中，刀剑的锋芒，灰姑娘的脚//维纳斯断臂的边缘"（长诗第九章）。这就是所谓的"残缺的美"。他像柏杨如数家"丑"般地写道——

"我们这个时代的诗人，脖子长的

叫小 a 小 b 小 c 小 d，脖子短些的

叫阿猫阿狗小鱼小虾。开始我们

光着屁股,整天一起打闹,后来
变声期时,一下子奔逃四散
谁也叫不出别人的名字。"

（长诗第三章）

这就是"陆健式"幽默,一是源自生活（包括生活中的某些具体细节,点点滴滴）,信手拈来,恰到好处;二是高度概括,言简意赅;三是语言炉火纯青,既妙趣横生,又耐人寻味。

3．拷问,从"呼救"开始（骨头的呼救）

在诗歌的语言及其生成层面,陆健同样遭遇了同代人"死亡阴影"的心理压力和语言焦虑。"但丁站在'A'字之尖顶上,俯视人类/的生路和死路;我站在'V'字的谷底/沉溺于深渊,向左边和右边呼救"（长诗第四章）。显然,这是由于一种深层危机而从骨子里发出来的呼救。

每天照例上演着语言的失效和死亡。当一首诗刚刚完成,便已死于信息的海洋,死于心灵的荒漠。只有不甘心沉沦、勇于担当的诗人,才会发出这种对语言的呼救,对自我的呼救,也是对诗的呼救!

A．自拆骨头和同道骨头 "有人说我故作严肃,作外国名士状/居室中到处张贴欧美名家语录/在大师的肩膀后面窥视世界"。"有人说/我面无表情,用脖子举着自己的画像//招摇过市。在汉语中夹杂拼音文字/我先天不足,不得不如此"（长诗第四章）——从大师肩膀上的胛骨（一称琵琶骨）到自己脖子里的颈椎骨,从"窥视"到"面无表情",陆健通过自拆骨头而看透了整个诗坛同道的骨头和底气。

B．骨头的成色或扮相:作秀 网络传媒的发展及大众文化的勃兴,伴随而来的是作秀成为一种时尚。一如"学术秀、真人秀、做秀、模仿秀/口齿伶俐秀、结结巴巴秀。作/沉思状、作假想状荒诞状、作//左半身右半身极不对称状/装嫩、装酷、装相、装死狗"（长诗第八章）。

从教育、文化乃至整个社会，由于利益至上的心理驱动而导致道德下滑，人性沉沦。"听听教育体制的绝望/捂住耳朵钻进草垛也能听见呼救"（长诗第十六章）。面对这一现实和现象，只有自省精神才能唤醒人类的良知及良心。正是陆健的这一有如志士般的自省精神，照亮了自己的骨头、语言和赤诚的诗行。"执起教鞭把知识的营养与毒素/均匀搅拌，灌进学生食道，换回/我的柴米油盐和深深的愧疚//多么平凡，却又惊心动魄！我/想起自己有意或无意给别人的/伤害，他们不是我的病友//就是我的亲人。"（长诗第十三章）

C.时间的骨头：缺钙→骨质疏松→宿命　时间和历史是无情的。我们作为人类文明的后来者和继承者，一方面是有幸的，另一方面则有着一种被文化宿命所预设、被基因定制和环境改写的双重不幸。正如陆健自己归纳的由"时间单位"生成的语言链条：从"营养单一"到"缺钙"，再由"骨质疏松"到"体质虚弱"（长诗第十一章）；以致"众多的基因被改写，生命在//萌芽中便丧失了活力"（长诗第十五章）。

陆健从不掩饰这一代诗人的尴尬和无奈。"古往今来来过无数人（文化先贤）"，他们中的"许多人"已深深地融入我们的血脉之中，并"再也没有消失过"。"他们哭、笑、得意、痛不欲生，曾经/忧虑或嘲笑我们。他们是我们的亲人//又与我们毫无关系。他们高大伟岸/有时又会从我们的指缝间漏走/他们用话语堵住我们的嘴巴"（长诗第一章）。

问题恰恰在于，这些文化先贤既是"我们的亲人"，又与"我们毫无关系"。之所以说他们是我们的"亲人"，是因为我们的血液中流动着他们的基因；之所以说他们与我们"毫无关系"，是因为我们不能在文化进化上一成不变地复制或重复他们。但是，由于这一基因的遮蔽性过于强大，这就给其后继者带来文化创新上无穷无尽的难题及危机。

是的，"假如一个民族优秀的大脑接踵病变/蛛网萦结，堕落倾圮，谎言恣肆"（长诗第十五章）；而"诗歌的手臂已经脱臼/她扶不起那个叫做现实的大脑袋"，"唯有自尊像一块还不太脏的粗布/我们用它做成旗子还是做成短裤？"（第二十一章下阕《记下我们对语言所犯的罪行》）陆健的诗歌命运，正是整个中国当代诗人族群的命运。我们仿佛听见他们的骨头与时间骨头的碰撞之声，听见他们在与自身的文化基因及当下语境秩序进行一场博弈和搏斗的刀兵相向之声。

三、风格：打造长诗艺术经典

（陆健独特的"泛叙实"式贡献）

"匮乏时代，诗人何为？"海德格尔的警言时时萦回在陆健的耳边。在当下这个非诗时代，诗歌及诗人的生存同样受到前所未有的严峻挑战！有人声称写诗的远比读诗的多，甚至认为"诗歌已死"。"人们研究文化，就频频意淫"（长诗第五章）。而作为有良知的知识分子（包括诗人）命定地总是与责任、良心同在，与善同在。据此，陆健在长诗的第六章毫不犹豫地写道："纵使世界已被拼贴成一张扁平的脸/诗人注定是那个挺身而出的鼻子"。一如美国诗人斯温逊在面对二十世纪中期口语化倾向（主要来自"垮掉派"和自白派两个诗群）笼罩着整个美国诗坛的时候，他的内心却始终是坚定和满怀自信的。他认为，只有"诗能够帮助人保持其人的本质。"[8]

从艺术本体论的层面上说，陆健的《一位美轮美奂的小诗人之歌》是一部向上仰望、向下忏悔的长诗，是一个诗人经历了深刻的心理危机，而后奋起，并向全社会发出警醒式呼唤的长诗，是诗人在与生活现实发生文化碰撞和语言磨擦后挣扎前行、孜孜探求的长诗，是中国诗坛继海子之后最纯粹和决绝的心灵救赎的长诗。在这部别开生面的长诗中，我们不难看出陆健日臻圆熟而独具个性魅力的艺术特色。

1. 经典式"宏大叙事"结构

这部长诗的成功首先得益于其精湛、典雅而具有建筑美的结构。可以说，陆健为苦心孤诣地打造这样一部长诗艺术经典，他此前至少做了 20 多年"泛叙实"诗的探索和准备。陆健从诗特写系列到纪实诗系列写作，实质上正是他写作这部具有"宏大叙事"性质长诗的一种"艺术热身"或前奏。

一方面，陆健将《神曲》三部曲（全诗共 14233 行）的鸿篇巨制结构微缩成 26 个英文字母的章节形式（全诗 702 行），另一方面又从诗歌的内容及思想题旨上将艾略特的"荒原"意识贯穿到底。陆健给自己的心理及诗学定位是："像弗罗斯特那样感知，感动，感恩"。"仔细丈量脚下道路的弗罗斯特/你摸到了生存的命脉，所以说出//你回到事物的根"；"行走在田埂/引颈仰望星空的无比辽阔//为卑微的人们和自己写下诗章/轻声颂祷，麦花香和上天的垂顾/日复一日在时间的肋骨穿过"（长诗第二十六章）。

诗的每一章均由"主题诗"（或称上阕）和"对题诗"（或称下阕）两部分组成，其中作为大写的"主题诗"共九行三小节，而作为复调形式的小写"对题诗"则是十八行六小节；同时，"对题诗"所带出的主题也可视为对"主题诗"的一种艺术延伸、变奏、呈示、发展和再现。这一由一奇（九行）、一偶（十八行）所组成的独特的诗行结构，无疑是对中国道家思想"一阴一阳"格局的借鉴及化用。

但丁在其《神曲》的"宏大叙事"中，不但涉及了古代社会生活的方方面面、林林总总，如政治、经济（含金融）、宗教、法律、教育、文化、艺术、历史、地理、自然灾害等。同时他还在诗中囊括了既往时代的众多人物。而陆健在《一位美轮美奂的小诗人之歌》中，除了作为每章标题的中外20多位名人，还在诗中表现了"我"及古今中外的众多人物。在其所表现的内容上，则涉及了政治、经济、教育、文化、艺术、法律、医学、爱情、伦理、道德、国民素质，甚至网络、超市、"盘峰论剑"、三鹿奶粉、强拆、裸聊、环保、物价问题等等，该关注的社会热点问题，陆健差不多全都涉及了。可以说，这部只有700多行的长诗几乎就是一部中国当代的风情录、人文史。长诗的最大成功，便是颇具匠心地用这一独一无二的结构将以上庞杂而互不关联的领域、范畴及一个个生活场面、细节囊括在一部作品里。透过它，我们可以看出一个学者型诗人博大深邃的思想脉络、艺术高度和难度，及其良苦用心。

2．复调手法和赋格体神韵

复调音乐（polyphony music）原指由几个声部构成的多声部音乐，相对于单声部音乐而言；后指按照对位法则结合在一起的多个旋律性声部的音乐，相对于主调音乐而言。复调音乐注重每个声部的旋律性，声部间形成对比或相互补充，没有主次之分。

陆健在这部长诗中，通过每章上阕主调与下阕复调的对位组合，并使诗的题旨时而交叉、时而重叠，从而形成了类似一问一答、一唱一和的二重唱式"宏大对话"。本来，在很多大型音乐作品中无不是以主调为主，而复调仅是起到一种辅助作用。但这部长诗的复调却在各章中不停地冲击着主调，诗人仿佛故意以一种外在的"非诗"因素不停地挤压严肃的诗歌主题，以世俗来调侃乃至亵渎崇高。此时的主调也许并不知道或者说有时已忘掉了自己是主调。一如整个人类文明史中，很多时期往往是由某种堕落因素主宰着世界，并悄悄地改变着世界历史的进程。

在长诗第二十章下阕《诗与时代，下行音阶》中，陆健这样写道："偶遇一首诗，偶遇一种心情/在湖州南浔古镇，在小莲庄/……抬头有气势非凡的牌匾"；"门内是什么摇弋着季节？/……举起西湖一样的绿伞、花朵/的粉红娇艳和杨万里的诗篇/我好似周朝的采诗官，吟唱/'荷叶田田'。"

我们知道，既有的诗歌审美传统已形成一种不成文的习惯——奇数诗行小节（段）为不稳定结构，偶数诗行小节（段）为稳定结构。据此，中外的诗歌建行多以四行为一段，因为它更有利于表达一种完整、稳定的情绪，并使之回环有度。陆健却一反这一诗美传统习惯，而以三行为一段（即奇数建段）。诗人之所以采用这一贯穿始终的诗行建筑，主要是源自其整部长诗的不稳定情绪的需要：一种失重而局促的精神状态。但从整体上看，它又像一个非常严谨的交响乐或歌剧结构，甚至更像一个讲求对称、在不稳定中以类似"对位法"的理念来达到平衡的建筑，中西合璧的雄伟建筑。

陆健仿若一个经验丰富的作曲家那样，娴熟地运用复调和赋格体手法，将主题加以各种不同的调性与节奏的变化，从而形成了统括全诗的关于"诗与生活、与诗人"这一重大的主题及核心形象。在诗歌美学层面上说，这一手法一是凸现了其结构的秩序性和完整性，二是具有复调音乐的对位、呼应效果，三是具有宗教音乐般的庄严华丽风格，四是为容易流于散乱的长诗提供了一个富有凝聚力的向心体式。

3．诸法杂糅的语言特色

这部长诗在语言文本上的实验也是绚丽多彩和富有成效的。诗中不但借鉴了具有两千多年传统的《诗经》"赋比兴"手法，而且从各个角度和层面对诗歌的语言进行了诸法杂糅的实验。其中包括象征性语言、超现实语言和关键性词语（或词象）的穿插、交叠，以及书面语和口语的融入、糅合。

陆健在诗中借奥斯卡·王尔德之口指出："这世界就是舞台，可角色分配得不像样子。"透过他的诗行，其语言机智可略见一斑："当今的伟大人物，就像被孩子//用草帽扣住的那只蚂蚱。""伟大只是穿行于人间的风，朴素而/敏感的心灵，绝望伸出的树叶般众多的/手，拽紧发疯的机车，到最后一分钟"（第十九章）。

在以上诗句中，陆健很经济地用了一个比喻词"（就）像"，便将"伟大"和"伟大人物"这一严肃的词汇及事物，一下子拉近了与"孩子""草帽""蚂蚱""人间的风"的空间距离及心理距离。紧接着，他又用"朴素而敏感的心灵""绝望伸出的树叶般众多的手"对"伟大"和"伟大人物"作了进一步的语言延伸和形象延伸。这几个句子既借用了比兴手法，又不留痕迹地将口语和书面语打磨成浑然一体的诗行。

又如长诗第十五章《中华民族到了最危险的时候》上阕，陆健蓦地将全诗的主题（音乐中称主导动机）在这里提高了八度："一百年来最伟大的汉语诗句/'最危险的时候'，一个民族/对准了一首诗歌的腰部//最危险的时候，不在 1911 年/不在 1937、1946、1989 年/在今天，就在我们面前"；"就在于信仰倒地，道德狼藉/即使天才创造出崭新的文体/所有锦绣文章也只能是病句"（长诗第十五章）。接下来，他将上阕"最危险的时候"这一关键性词语，在下阕开头三个小节的末行延伸成同一个诗句："一个民族就到了最危险的时候"，这既对题目作了呼应，又使小节与小节之间形成了一种排比关系；接着他又在第五个小节中，再次嵌入了这一诗句，使"最危险"的意象起到一种复沓的修辞效果，并与后面"语言成了喘息/韵脚成了垃圾，翻滚着，弥漫着"的句子融为一体。这一关键性词语（词象）在诗中的成功穿插和交叠，一方面是对语词的修辞功能的强化，另一方面则是对诗歌意象的深化和升华。

陆健俨然是一位语言的魔术师。他信手拈来，挥洒自如，从粮食、爱情、生育、校院、病房、读书、社交……等日常生活细节，写到诗歌创作、诗的语言及诗坛现状。长诗凸现了语言及语词本身的色彩、情味、节奏、语感，诗句长短之间的对比、平衡及和谐，注意语词的密度搭配以及谐音、近义、反义的结构组合，使语言切入生活的肌里及诗的细胞，并能保持语词与诗的鲜活、灵动、绚丽，让词的原生力量和金属穿透力得到最大限度的释放。

4．妙趣横生的幽默风格

除此之外，值得一提的，是陆健诗中妙趣横生的幽默风格。例如，他在长诗第二十五章上阕《科学是试错，人生也是》中这样写道："我曾扑身跌倒，被某种念头推拒/一股冲动，两缕情绪，三个词/没说出的话，半拉貌似新鲜的比喻//使我流血。那次无辜的行径像罪恶/语句的模棱两可——差点卖了本人/意象的陷阱，和摇摇欲坠的篇章结构"（长诗第二十五章）。

他先写自己曾经"扑身跌倒"，并被"某种念头推拒"，接着，心中涌起"一股冲动，两缕情绪，三个词"和"没说出的话"，以及"半拉貌似新鲜的比喻"。但谁也没有想到，正是上面的这些"冲动""情绪""词"和"话"，竟会使"我""流血"。

再看长诗第二十三章："我们所有的诗人都是小人物/我们的我们加起来成为一个/残缺不全的大诗人。博尔赫斯//已从容抵达，我们还在路上"。前面说，"我们的我们"（小人物）加起来，只能成为一个"残缺不全的大诗人"；后面则说博尔赫斯"已从容抵达"，而我们，竟"还在路上"。

在长诗第十九章，陆健更用一种自我调侃的口吻写道："此刻的我"，"不过是我大半生光阴的一个碎片/我满把的诗像十根手指不一般齐/它们概莫能外——终将零落成泥"。他的这一充满语言机智的幽默风格俯拾即是，是长诗中生动、风趣而富有张力的另一特色。让人读了，常常会忍不住发出会意的微笑（关于陆健诗歌的幽默风格，本文的第一部分也时有论及）。

"胸中几云梦，余地多恢宏。"（苏轼《次韵程正辅游碧落洞》）陆健是一位学者型且兼具多种艺术于一身的诗人。近年来，他的诗歌创作总是使人眼前一亮。他在诗的本质、诗的语言、诗与生活的关系等诗学问题上，也很有自己的独特见解。如果说，陆健在新世纪以来连续推出几部"泛叙实"力作《非典时期的了了特特博士》（2003 年 6 月）、《34 份礼物》（2004 年 5 月）、《田楼，田楼》（2006 年 10 月）、《枫叶上的比尔》（2006 年 6 月）、《洛水之阳》（2007 年 4 月）、《四方步》（2008 年 3 月），是他在 1992 年同时出版三部诗集《不存在的女子》《名城与门》《日内瓦的太阳》之后沉寂了 10 年"突然苏醒"的连锁性爆发；那么，陆健写毕于 2012 年 9 月的《一位美轮美奂的小诗人之歌》，则是一次具有新诗诗体建设意义的质变飞跃。他创造性地将但丁的胸怀、视野与艾略特的敏锐、深刻糅合在一起，向中国诗歌殿堂敬献上这部经典长诗。

应当指出，陆健的诗歌探索是成功的——尤其是这部接近无技巧境界的精湛长诗，堪称中国当代长诗的艺术精品，是新叙事主义时期诗歌的典范和代表性诗作。陆健正是凭着自己对诗歌及对知识分子立场的坚持，以一种"守望者"身份废寝忘食地不懈探索，并身体力行地把泛叙实诗派（The "Narration- related Verse " School）[9]的艺术手法及其元素贯穿到他的整个诗歌创作活动中，由此经历了集约式写作、最底层平民立场（为真实生存状态下的当代农民造像）、幽默风格的泛用、经典诗歌的精神移植等卓有成效的阶段性艺术实践，为中国新诗提供了一个成功的文本范例及"陆健现象"。

2013 年 3 月 17 日，于广州

注:

[1]诗特写（Poetry feature），指以诗的形式而化用电影艺术中"特写镜头"的表现手法来反映社会生活的一种新的体裁。其特点是抓住现实生活中的人物或事件的某一富有特征性部分，进行集中、精细、突出的描绘和刻画，具有高度的真实性和强烈的艺术感染力。这一诗歌体裁为陆健首创。

纪实诗（Documentary poetry），指以诗的形式如实地反映现实生活或历史中的真实人物与真实事件的体裁。由于诗歌自身的艺术特质及语言特性，纪实诗与纪实小说、叙事诗、报告文学等又有着本质的区别。笔者首次以"纪实诗"这一概念指称陆健的纪实性系列诗歌作品。以上概念及定义为笔者首创。

[2]赋格(英：fugue，德：fuge，法：fugue，意：fuga)一词的来源有多种说法，一般认为来自拉丁语，原意是"追逐"和"飞翔"。赋格曲的特点主要是相互模仿的声部在不同的音高和时间相继进入，按照对位法组成对应的乐句、形象，而形成各个声部相互问答追逐的效果。从 16 世纪的宗教音乐起直到 18 世纪的巴赫时代，赋格体音乐的艺术达到了顶峰。

对位，是指把两个或几个有关而独立的旋律合成一个单一的和声结构，而每个旋律又保持它自己的线条或横向的旋律特点。

[3]一译"吉约姆•阿波利奈尔"（Guillaume Apollinaire，1880－1918），法国 20 世纪第一位诗人，也是最著名的大诗人之一。他是未来主义的代表，又是超现实主义的先导。在其短促的一生中，他参与了 20 世纪初法国文学艺术领域中风靡一时的所有先锋派运动，并把诗歌引向未曾探索过的领域，对整个现代派诗歌具有巨大而深远的影响。柳鸣九称阿波利奈尔是"20 世纪诗歌道路上一位勇敢的开拓者"，"一个以其才情、智慧、敏锐、开创精神以及远见的理论视野，指引着 20 世纪诗歌新潮流的人物"。

[4]"蝴蝶效应"（The Butterfly Effect）是指在一个动力系统中，初始条件下微小的变化能带动整个系统的长期、巨大的连锁反应。这一效应学说促进了混沌学、系统生态学、基因学、气象学、逻辑学、股票市场学、测度论、泛函分析学、拓扑学、分形几何学等学科理论的发展。

[5]酸性体质血钙偏低(正常人的血钙指标是 2.18~2.63 毫摩尔/升,低于这一指标属缺钙),致使骨质疏松(osteoporosis),是一种以单位体积内骨组织量减少为特点的代谢性骨病变。

[6]一译"贝亚德",但丁的精神恋人及其长诗《神曲》中的人物,在作品中,她从猛兽面前营救但丁脱险,引领但丁走出迷途森林,后与但丁一起游历了天堂。

[7]镫骨,人耳的三个听小骨之一,形状像马镫,外面跟砧骨相连,位于鼓膜后面的中耳腔内,体积只有 2.6~3.4 毫米,重量仅为 2~4.3 毫克。

[8]见《诗人谈诗——二十世纪中期美国诗论》第 244 页,三联书店1989 年 8 月第 1 版。彼时的美国诗坛,"垮掉派"诗人惯用声嘶力竭的愤怒嚎叫把生活中的污秽、混乱和不人道现象赤裸地表现出来;而自白派诗人则以惊人的坦白方式把个人稳私、内心创伤、性欲、甚至自杀冲动等等全部公诸于众。这两个诗派对诗歌的口语化倾向无疑起到推波助澜的作用。

[9]泛叙实诗派（The "Narration- related Verse" School）,是指先后活跃于二十世纪八、九十年代中国诗坛,而于九十年代初汇聚在中国新诗讲习所(北京旧鼓楼大街西绦胡同 13 号西门),并以《中外诗星》《中国诗人报》等诗歌报刊为阵地的青年诗人群体。代表性诗人有祁人、陆健、子午(即呢喃,以上三人为发起人)、田原、洪烛、王明韵、阎志。此外,还有一批陆续来京寻梦的文学青年如商震、潘红莉、北塔等,以不同方式与前者保持着长期、稳定的诗歌及生活联系,继续探讨诗学问题,也属这个诗歌流派的成员(具体情形参见笔者《泛叙实诗派的由来及其艺术宗旨》一文,引自拙著《泛叙实诗派诗人论》,中国文联出版社 2013年版;或五国学者编选的《中国当代流派诗选》,中国文联出版社 2011年 8 月版)。

子午,本名许燕良,广州某文学研究院专业作家兼文论家,文化学者,中国作家协会会员,中国电影家协会会员,中国戏剧家协会会员,混语版《世界诗人》艺术顾问。

那些能够杀伤作者的作品

——诗集《一位美轮美奂的小诗人之歌》代后记

陆 健

作家和他的作品是什么关系？母子关系？"我"生出了另外一个"我"？作品完成之后作为一个"独立存在"到读者那里去了，和"我"没关系了？都对。那么作者在创作作品时他们是什么关系呢？好的作品——仅仅是足够好的触及到人类血脉的作品，这关系是作品在被写作过程中不断杀伤作者的关系。

并非在写《一位美轮美奂的小诗人之歌》（见《中国诗歌》2013年 3 期）时我才开始注意这个问题，也许因为愚钝，我想过很久。1991 年底的《重看曹禺话剧》一诗中，我认为曹禺的艺术，是"从我们的血肉中/抓出一把诗句"（文化艺术出版社 1992 年 9 月版拙著《名城与门》79 页）。欣赏的过程尚且如此，创作当甚之。"这艺术何用/令我冥顽而专心，我因为它/而把自己逼上绝路"（见人民文学出版社 2002 年 5 月版《中华诗歌百年精华》528 页拙作《向自己倾诉》）。意思是我终于能够说出一点"属于自己的"东西，是在人生到了濒临"绝路"的时候。面对文森特梵高，1991 年 8 月在《仓皇的向日葵》（见《十月》杂志 1995 年 3 期，台湾诗之华出版社 1992 年10 月版《日内瓦的太阳》34 页）中我写道，"我的疼痛无边涌荡/天才是人类的疾病"。有艺术才能的人的一个重要功能就是抵达对同类的痛苦与欢乐的感受极限并能够以人们熟知的手段加以表现，假如不意间突破了这极限，就只有疯掉。我至今还能清楚回忆起当时写这首诗时内火攻心、气血逼喉的情景。梵高在法国阿尔作画时想必有过之无不及。同样地，《日瓦戈医生》的作者帕斯捷尔纳克如此，写了《1984年》的奥威尔如此。歌德写《浮士德》被它折磨了六十年，陈忠实被《白鹿原》淘空了身子，再也不写大篇幅的作品，曹雪芹和《红楼梦》同时害着一场大病，结果《红楼梦》胜出——它还没被写完，作者就被熬死了。小说由高鹗续写，曹雪芹却无法活转来。更有梁山伯与祝英台用真正的行为艺术书写了他们前无古人的绝版爱情，浪漫主义诗人海子从诗歌的幽径"走到了人类的尽头"在山海关引颈自杀。这样的例子非常多，这是命运，"它的大小就是我们的大小"（见《一位美轮美奂的小诗人之歌》章节M"掀开命运的纸牌"）。有的作家被击伤，侥幸有命，比如《废都》之后的贾平凹、《檀香刑》之后的莫言。不是说他们的精神自我修复能力超强，而是这些作品还不是可以用来兑换自己生命的作品，这些还不是从他们的骨髓中提炼出来的就他而言最伟大的作品。伟大的作品在期待中在不可知中。我们看到整部文学史、艺术史，就是作家、艺术家们的殒命史。

几乎所有触及读者心灵最深处，在极大程度上反映了人的本质存在的作品，对于创作这作品的的人都有一定杀伤力。作者释放，消耗，疲惫，喋血，虚脱，大脑被洗劫一空，智力下降，精神失重，不清楚自己还有没有力气有没有价值。若要写下一部书，需要重头做起——知识与经验积累、智力水平、技艺，高手被自己陌生化了，似乎自己的生命归零了。为什么？

这些作品开启了一个秘密通道，让人窥见了生存的一些幽奥。这幽奥是常人几乎无一例外地患有白内障的肉眼看不到的。这幽奥近乎天机，中国古人云："天机不可泄露。"看见那真理强光的眼睛一定会受伤。"天妒英才"，不是妒，人力所及的一切都不值得嫉妒，上帝在不经意之间、不曾发力就挫败了他。上帝也许是个巨大的黑洞，你和他接通，获得能量的同时你的能量也被吸摄走了。我一直有一个模糊的感觉，艺术家比科学家更容易冒犯上帝。在上帝巨大的尺幅中，科学家认知的刻度很具体，上帝看得很清楚。艺术家痛苦、纠结，头顶一团火光或雾气，上帝有时也不知道他在做什么——看来人类的愚蠢不是那么单纯——使他有点烦，最终要让人间的"艺术家"付出代价。释迦牟尼成佛，以遮蔽净饭王王子为代价，上帝造人，他没死，竟也只能以牺牲自己的儿子来让人读懂自己浩瀚的内心，难道人间的艺术家可以轻轻松松分泌作品，他难道在对他人施加影响的过程中比神祇更有优先权吗？

也许以上都是妄念，妄言。"人类一思考，上帝就发笑。"因为人在思考关于上帝的事情，像一群蚂蚁谈论河外星系。但思考人间的事情，上帝就不一定发笑了。若是连人间自己的事情都不肯思考，岂不是懒惰到无法原谅？于是乎科学家艺术家殚精竭虑，纷纷然展现自己的聪明，或欣欣然、戚戚然探讨生存问题，描述世相，表达自己的痛苦、快乐的情感。科学家、艺术家产生了。

在这儿我应该试举《一位美轮美奂的小诗人之歌》的写作为例。显然，它不是一部带有神性的作品，而是人间烟火气很浓的作品。是要解决"当今之世，诗人何为"的问题。我们知道，诗歌不是常常作为解决具体问题的手段的，屈原的《天问》也只提出疑问。"小诗人之歌"仰望天庭，俯瞰大地，四顾茫茫，试图像自己希望的那样生活、写作。"纵使天才创造出崭新的文体/所有锦绣文章也只能是病句"（《小诗人之歌》章节０"高悬之剑"），他清楚，但毕竟不甘心，他想接近"美轮美奂"——借助建筑学的一个中国词汇——自己能力范围内的最佳状态，可自己却百病缠身，烦恼无尽，传统文人和现代诗人的毛病他都有。现在，他必须和自己算算账，把自己摊开在太阳下面，看看到底有多少病灶。他需要面对太多的问题：人性的弱点，一叶障目的主观视角，患得患失的价值取向，期望世俗成功的虚荣心，软弱，懒惰，缺乏信仰、担当，随波逐流诸如此类。他与他的诗歌同外部世界的关系，包括信仰问题，中西文化传统的借鉴吸收问题，自我与社会的关系问题，纷乱世相及其救助的可能性，还有诗人与诗歌的关系，与语言的关系，等等，线索繁多，难以抽丝剥茧。这就是为什么一首仅仅七百多行的诗歌竟耗费了我将近六年时光的原因。我有拿六年生命去和一首诗进行兑换的决心，可既然"所有锦绣文章也只能是病句"，这首诗难道可以有另外一种结局吗？

我想《一位美轮美奂的小诗人之歌》的作者起码是诚实的。具体体现在，一，我们处在历史——时间纵轴的一个点上，前贤巍峨，我们今天的一切都和他们有关，他们至今没有离开过我们，只要我们想到他们，他们就会出现。他们仍旧会借助我们的大脑思考，借助我们的身体感受，甚至他们的思维与表述，多年前就跑到我们现在的前面去了。《小诗人之歌》不仅从他们的思想中得到营养，接着他们的话往下说，试图提供一个"艺术家当下状态的独特诗歌文本"。在这首诗中，通过引用的方式，前贤们似乎团结了起来，为《小诗人之歌》构成了一个形式上的稳定结构。这些都强化了本诗作者的自信，使他相信这次诗歌之旅是得到了前人的帮助的，此次写作会是一次有益（哪怕是"试错"）的尝试，不会空手而返。同时前贤们在此给作者设置了一个高大的壁垒，逼迫作者与他们"平视着说话"，因为他的志向是"在前贤止步的地方起笔"（见《小诗人之歌》章节 C "不是毛笔，也不是鹅毛笔"）。这对任何当代诗人都不是一个很低的要求。从宏观视域观之，诗歌绝非个人能够独立成就，是古往今来的所有人在写着同一部关于人类的作品，所有个人的才华、努力、产品，均不足挂齿。这一点《小诗人之歌》的作者是清楚的，因此他的姿态，或者说在诗中的位置，不在任何一位前贤之下，也不在"街角窃笑的女郎"之上。他在——在现场，他思——前贤之意，他感受——世态、自我，他说出——使所在、所思、所感形成一个话语场；二，为了向前贤表示敬意，向读者表示诚意，《小诗人之歌》所涉及的具体人物、具体事件也几乎都是真实的。就诗歌的一般创作规律而言，除了纪实性较强的史诗、诗报告之外，诗中的人物、事件是否真实并不重要，但《小诗人之歌》有意坚持"真实性原则"，作者的社会职业、家庭与情感生活等等。这些就是构成他的"个人史诗"的基础和要素，对个人真实经历、生活的描述过程中，在"临在"情境中，作者的感情才会更在"状态"。这真实使得诗人不向任何社会力量与任何个人低头，迎风流泪不以为羞。那些"三缄其口"的谨慎、"谦谦君子"的文雅、虚幻的荣誉追求，统统不在话下。不给所有人（包括自己）留下情面，不为尊者讳，不为贤者讳。毁誉由人；三，诗歌语言的混成状态。《小诗人之歌》中有文言文（主要见诸引文部分），有书面语，口语。诗歌好与不好，和使用什么样的语言关系并不直接，必须依据诗歌本身的需要。就《小诗人之歌》而言，它需要一个消化能力比较强的胃。我们面对的是以往人类的全部精神成果，是当今混乱不堪的世界与中国口水横流的现实的全部以及诗人千疮百孔的人生，语义杂陈，语法混乱，它们拥挤在诗人的思维里，发言为诗，不"泥沙俱下"才怪。因之混成状态定是作者遵从"真实"的原则的有意为之，包括时而爆出粗口——回送必须爆粗口的事物的恰如其分的言辞表达。

我很服膺单占生先生在《陆健诗歌的心路历程》一文中对我本人创作的时期划分，我甚至愿意将《一位美轮美奂的小诗人之歌》之前的所有写作都看作"实习阶段"。单占生说，在此之前，"陆健对人与社会、人与宇宙的认识还是分离的，人就是人，世界就是世界。而到了《一位美轮美奂的小诗人之歌》，在诗人和这位美轮美奂的小诗人面前，人与这个世界就再也不能分开了，人就是这个世界的全部。"尽管不少批评家对陆健上世纪 90 年代初的《名城与门》《日内瓦的太阳》，本世纪初的《温暖》等诗集曾给与相当的认可和关注。当然，即使对《小诗人之歌》也有不同看法，比如一位著名刊物的诗歌编辑直言不喜欢，认为它是典型的"知识分子写作"文本，所有知识分子写作的特征它都有，"现在谁还这么写诗啊？"一位网友认为他宁肯去读口水诗，老妪能诵才是可取的。而我历来对"知识分子写作"这个概念存有疑虑的，认为写作不能过于强调知识和所谓智慧，不能只用脑袋写诗，要有整个身体的体验来参与。同时写作要有难度，规模较大的作品一定要有与之相适应的整体设计，形式架构。解构现实现象、近乎口语化的东西我当然也不乏尝试，比如"21 世纪的道德已经失去了高山的崔巍/传统像一只旧船，甲板、桨橹破碎/点燃成火，也冷了最后的茶炊/话语权是大众的衣领围圈起来/缝制成的频频更换的漱口杯/离岸已远，往事难追/咱们的幸福生活，就这样被拖下水//你白我也白，你黑咱也黑，谁都别说谁/你拉我就推，你填咱就堆，谁都别怪谁/曰官、曰民、曰匪，指的是旧社会/上帝堕落，法律犯罪，是后现代审美/花拳绣腿，不赚不赔，惭愧惭愧/咱们的幸福生活，就是我把你拖下水/你把我拖下水，咱们把大家/大家把咱们全都拖下水"（拙作《咱们的幸福生活》见 2005 年 12 期《星星》诗刊）。于此可见，我就是我，不愿去"作谁""像谁"。这就是历次诗歌思潮、流派都与我无关的原因吧？希姆博尔斯卡说，假如写诗是无聊的话，那么，"写诗的无聊和不写诗的无聊比较起来，我还是愿意选择前者"。生存是痛苦的，写诗的痛苦和不写诗的痛苦比较起来，我也选择前者。我是诗歌的一个学徒，甘心情愿接受它的击打。我的理想是以有生之年"与微不足道的诗句交换手稿"（见《小诗人之歌》章节 z "夜间的颂祷"），被时光之手轻轻拿起轻轻放下。"这世上只有诗篇，没有诗人"（见《小诗人之歌》章节 w "我曾想，但没做到，我仍在想"）。我们的所谓"才华"，没那么重要。其实我们有没有才华还不一定呢。

2013 年 4 月 1 日，北京

（原载诗集《一位美轮美奂的小诗人之歌》明天出版社 2013 年 12月版）

作者介绍

陆健，祖籍陕西扶风，1956 年出生于河北沧州，在河南洛阳读完中小学，南阳插队 4 年半，1978 年考入北京广播学院，在中央电台、河南省文联曾有任职，现为中国传媒大学教授，已退休。1991 年加入中国作家协会。

主要出版书籍

诗集《红十字下面的祈祷》1989 年 5 月海燕出版社

诗集《窗户嘹亮的声音》，1990 年 11 月新加坡文化学术协会

诗集《美丽的大风之夜》（与易殿选合著）1991 年 3 月花山文艺出版社

诗集《不存在的女子》1992 年 8 月香港金陵书社出版公司

诗集《名城与门》，1992 年 9 月文化艺术出版社

诗集《日内瓦的太阳》，1992 年 10 月台湾诗之华出版社

诗集《陆健诗选》，1998 年 10 月中国文联出版公司

诗集《非典时期的了了特特博士》，2003 年 6 月春风文艺出版社

文学评论集《20 世纪外国著名短诗 101 首赏析》，2003 年 7 月珠海出版社

诗集《34 份礼物》，2004 年 5 月北京广播学院出版社

诗集《七次话语》，2005 年 11 月沈阳出版社

诗集《枫叶上的比尔》，2006 年 8 月深圳海天出版社

诗集《马赛克拼图》，2006 年 9 月作家出版社

诗集《田楼，田楼》，2006 年 10 月中州古籍出版社

诗集《洛水之阳》，2007 年 4 月河南文艺出版社

文艺评论集《影像，心象》，2007年11月陕西人民出版社

诗集《四方步》，2008年3月香港美术市场出版社

诗集《温暖》，2008年12月辽宁人民出版社

诗集《一位美轮美奂的小诗人之歌》，2013年12月明天出版社

诗集《一些片段》，2014年6月中国广播电视出版社

诗集《诗坛N叟》2014年11月线装书局

诗集《思想起》2017年12月河南文艺出版社

诗集《洛水之阳》（增订本）2021年1月郑州大学出版社

诗集《开片——2020年诗选》2021年7月郑州大学出版社

诗集《短长》2022年12月中国诗书画出版社

诗集《陆健长诗选》2023年12月中国诗书画出版社

诗集《陆健域外题材诗选》2023年12月中国诗书画出版社

诗集《北方之南，南方之北》2023年12月百花洲文艺出版社

诗集《我称之为光明》2024年8月辽宁人民出版社

获奖情况

诗歌《海的向往》1982年获《飞天》"首届大学生诗苑奖"

诗歌《在天上，在岸边，在水里》1985年获首届《诗神》杂志优秀作品奖

诗歌《三个士兵和他们的胡子》获1985年《星星》诗歌奖

诗歌《仓皇的向日葵》获1995年《十月》文学奖

组诗《二十世纪的故事》获1999年《人民文学》年度奖

组诗《诗坛N叟》2011年获《大河诗歌》杂志"首届大河主编诗歌奖"

组诗《是母亲节救了我的母亲》2013年获《诗刊》首届"中国（文成）刘伯温诗歌奖"

组诗《<温暖的雪>和它前面的诗》2013年获《中国作家》第三届郭沫若诗歌奖三等奖

长诗《一位美轮美奂的小诗人之歌》2014年获中国诗歌学会首届"中国屈原诗歌奖银奖"

诗集《一位美轮美奂的小诗人之歌》2014年获广东首届"中国阮章竞诗歌奖"首奖

诗集《一位美轮美奂的小诗人之歌》2014年获"首届中国（佛山）长诗奖"

诗集《一位美轮美奂的小诗人之歌》2018年获第二届"昌耀诗歌奖"

长诗《病妻》2019年获《诗参考》"中国30年优秀长诗奖"

陆健诗歌研究论文集

《关于一个诗人》晓雪、张同吾、陆健等著，1997年2月百花文艺出版社；

《诗篇，向经典致敬》2014年4月线装书局。

译者介绍

Denis Mair（梅丹理），美国诗人，中英文翻译者，俄亥俄州立大学中文硕士。曾担任台湾涵静学院研究员，美国宾州大学东亚语文系讲师，北京中坤基金翻译顾问。译作包括真华法师《参学琐谭》（纽约州立大学出版社，1992）、冯友兰《三松堂全集自序》（夏威夷大学出版社，2000）、朱朱《一幅画的诞生》（湖南美术出版社）。诗歌翻译包括《麦城诗选》（伦敦 Shearsman Books，2009）；马悦然编《台湾新诗选》（哥仑比雅大学出版社，2005）；狄马加《黑色狂欢曲》（俄克拉荷马大学出版社，2014）；吉狄马加《群山的影子》（南非姆基瓦出版社，2014）、骆英《文革记忆》（俄克拉荷马大学出版社，2015）；吉狄马加《从雪豹到马雅科夫斯基》（旧金山 Kallatumba Press，2017）；杨克《地球苹果的两半》（俄克拉荷马大学出版社，2017）；还有骆英《7+2登山日记》（白松出版社）。他翻译的当代诗人还包括严力、孟浪等。其个人英文诗集《木刻里的人》于 2004 年由洛杉矶 Valley Contemporary Poets 出版。

www.ingramcontent.com/pod-product-compliance
Lightning Source LLC
Chambersburg PA
CBHW021227130626
46554CB00004B/1400